THE

CULTURAL

TSUNAMI

Preparing Your Child To Stand Against
The Coming Wave

By: Patty Frey Nelson

PRESS

Deut 6:4-7

Patty M

*This book is dedicated to my husband, Paul,
my true life partner,*

*our children, Christopher, Rebecca Meyer,
Michelle and Heather*

and our sweet grand-daughter Lillie Grace.

I am so thankful that God put all of you in my life.

You are an undeserved blessing!

TABLE OF CONTENTS

ACKNOWLEDGEMENTS

This book is a labor of love and would not have been possible without the support, patience and encouragement of my family every step of the way. Paul, you have supported every dream I have imagined since we met when I was 18 years old. I am so grateful to God for you! Chris, Rebecca, Michelle and Heather, you have loved me unconditionally, forgiven my shortcomings and challenged me to pursue my dreams. My dear parents Robert and Hazel Frey, my sweet sister Kimberly Barnes and my dear mother-in-law Shirley Nelson have been a constant source of love and encouragement. Amanda Holland and Alison Vacek patiently reviewed sections of this book with an editor's eye to find grammatical and spelling errors and to offer suggestions for wording and readability. My dear friend Susanne Vacek carefully read the manuscript and offered insightful suggestions and encouragement. Thank you so much to all of you! You are each a blessing from God!

With joy,
Patty Frey Nelson

SO WHO IS PATTY NELSON AND WHY SHOULD I READ THIS BOOK?

R ight up front I feel compelled to address those of you who have picked up this book and are perusing it to determine if it is worth reading. If you are looking for a book written by someone who has it all together as a parent and has raised children who have it all together, you may wish to return this book to the shelf and move on. I do not pretend to have all the answers. I am a flawed person who has experienced many ups and downs throughout the 30 plus years that I have been a parent. My children have had their share of struggles in life, many of which they could blame on me if they were so inclined.

This book comes from a sincere heart that feels deep compassion for the struggles of parents and teenagers. I have personally experienced many of the agonies and made many of the mistakes that I will talk about in this book. I have learned so much about myself in this journey called "parenting."

I was a stay-at-home mother for 17 years and have been working as a mental health therapist for 12 years. For a few years, I worked in a program that sent therapists into the homes of families in crisis as a last ditch attempt to keep families together. I also worked as a School Therapist (not the same thing as a guidance counselor). I had offices at inner-city elementary and middle schools. Kids were referred to my office during the school day for counseling regarding personal and home life issues that were interfering with their ability to function at school. You'd be amazed at the big problems little elementary-aged children carry around with them. I currently work as an Outpatient Therapist specializing in adolescents and teens and their families. I have volunteered as a youth group leader and Sunday School teacher for several years as well. Call me crazy, but I love teenagers.

My intent in writing this book is to share from my heart what I have learned as a parent, therapist and youth worker in hopes of bringing insight, encouragement and practical strategies to parents and those who work with adolescents, teens and young adults. My reason for writing it now is the profound changes I have seen in the past several years in the teenage culture in America. It is my belief that a vast majority of this generation of young people is at risk of being lost in every way a person can be lost.

That may seem like an extreme statement; however, I do not believe it is an overstatement. This generation of young people has grown up in a world with few firm, immovable boundaries. A restriction is often seen as something to evade, and respect for authority is practically non-existent. Teenagers often demand explanations for every rule with which they are presented, and if they disagree with the explanation, they don't believe they are required to obey. They will obey a rule if they have come to the conclusion that the consequence for breaking the rule is too great to risk, not because they respect the authority that created or is enforcing the rule. This is a very important distinction.

This generation is also engaging in self-destructive behaviors like never before. The downward slide began a couple generations back, as described by Dr. James Dobson of Focus on the Family Ministries. In his book *Dare to Discipline*, published in 1970, Dr. Dobson describes this downward slide in this way:

"At last in post-war America, 1950-1970, a generation was born on which all the coveted goodness was heaped. But instead of bringing exuberance and gratitude, there has come antagonism and haughty contempt for the generation that worked to provide it. Why?. . . . the central cause of the turmoil among the young must again be found in the tender years of childhood: we demanded neither respect nor responsible behavior from our children, and it should not be surprising that some of our young citizens are now demonstrating the absence of these virtues."[1]

The generation of children he was describing includes most of the parents raising the current generation. It is easy to see where the disrespect began. Dr. Dobson believes in a balanced approach to parenting, where neither authoritarianism nor permissiveness is exclusively practiced by parents. He explains his conclusions this way:

"The pendulum has swept back and forth regularly between harsh, oppressive discipline and the unstructured permissiveness of the 1950s. It is time that we realize that both extremes leave their characteristic scars on the lives of young victims, and I would be hard pressed to say which is more damaging."[2]

I completely agree with his assessment.

****

I have come to the conclusions presented in this book from the perspective of a wife, a stay-at-home mother of four, a Sunday School teacher, a youth worker, a family therapist, and a casual observer at my local Wal Mart. Each of these perspectives is interwoven into the pages of this book. As stated earlier, my desire is to impart the knowledge and insight that I have gained through my experiences and observations to empower today's parents to raise children who will challenge the *Cultural Tsunami,* which I will describe in the following section. I also want to help parents gain insight into the teenage culture to help them understand why they may be facing issues with their teenagers that make no sense to them as parents. I will offer suggestions as to different approaches that have proven to be effective in my own personal parenting and in the lives of others whom I have counseled.

I have an eclectic therapeutic approach. I believe there are times to draw on varying psychological theories. I was educated in secular institutions. Some Christians who have come to me for counsel have expressed concern about that part of my resume. My answer to their concerns is that I do not believe that the teaching of how human beings typically function is inaccurate simply because it is taught in a secular institution by a non-Christian. The information learned by medical doctors in secular institutions regarding the physical functioning of the human brain or body is no less accurate when it is taught by non-believers in non-Christian institutions. I believe the same is true of information regarding how individuals typically function in the non-physical realm.

As Christians we are to use the *Holy Bible* and the guidance of the Holy Spirit as our filters for all information we take into our hearts and minds. I do not adhere to any one psychological theory exclusively and I believe there is a danger in becoming too rigid when dealing with the complexities of human behavior. The one absolute on which I will not waiver is the authority of Scripture. I filter every parenting philosophy and psychological theory that I come across through the truth of God's Word and the foundational belief that we are all born with a sinful nature. In support of this belief, Genesis 8:21 says that after Noah and his family had safely come out of the ark and made an altar to God:

"The LORD smelled the pleasing aroma and said in his heart: "Never again will I curse the ground because of humans, even though every inclination of the human heart is evil from childhood."[3]

Jeremiah 17:9 says: "The heart is deceitful above all things and beyond cure. Who can understand it?"[4] We may wish to believe that all of humanity, especially newborn babies, is basically good until corrupted by the world. Unfortunately, that is not the case. I believe, based on Scripture and supported by my own experiences and observations, that we begin this life as self-centered beings that need to be trained to rein in our evil desires and tendencies. I did not have to teach my children to say no to me at 18 months old. Defying me and behaving selfishly came as easily for them as breathing. The prolific novelist Taylor Caldwell expressed this belief very clearly in her 1971 memoir *On Growing Up Tough*:

> "I do believe in remembering that children are naturally infirm so far as acceptable virtue is concerned, and that they are not "delicate" and precious little blossoms as some of the child worshipers assert. Virtue in children, and civic responsibility, is something that must be taught painfully by stern parents and sterner teachers. Children do not come by it naturally, being human."[5]

I have developed my own foundational theory of parenting that addresses what I believe to be the number one problem in our standard approach to child-rearing today. I will describe this "Brick Wall of Authority" in detail in a later chapter.

Training up a child to be a positive influence on the world around him is extremely important; however, the Holy Spirit within a person, through a relationship with Jesus Christ, is the only hope for deep, personal transformation. Our most important responsibility as parents is to show our children the way to Jesus through teaching, training and, most importantly, our own example.

My primary perspective on everything in life is that of a devoted follower of Jesus Christ. God is not just a concept in my life – He is my life. "In Him [I] live and move and have [my] being."[6] I ask Him for wisdom and guidance every day and encourage you to do the same. The book of James tells us "If

xv

any of you lacks wisdom, he should ask God, who gives generously to all without finding fault, and it will be given to him."[7] I will be offering biblical references throughout this book to reinforce my words, as I believe that God Himself gives us the perfect example of parenting. He is generous with words of encouragement, help, and caution throughout the Scriptures.

I would strongly discourage anyone from attempting to apply the strategies in this book to extreme family situations where abuse is being perpetrated. Emotional, psychological, verbal, or physical abuse is never acceptable and must be identified and dealt with first before the guidance and principles in this book can be effectively applied. The safety of children must be established in the home first and foremost. Our children need and deserve to know that they are valued and protected before we can expect them to respond to the strategies put forth in these pages. A child (or adult for that matter) coming out of abuse needs individualized, intensive, one-on-one attention to guide them through the healing process.

Before we begin this journey I need to share with you the disclaimer that I tell parents who come into my office. You are the parent of your child. You are responsible for your children, just as my husband and I were responsible for raising ours. I will make suggestions and put forth strategies in this book but it is up to you to exercise the discernment and wisdom of God in determining how to best deal with your own children. You know them and you know your own personal family situation. Ask God for wisdom, use the brain He gave you, and seek the guidance of godly people you trust. Then parent boldly! My message to parents is to be fearless, never give up and lean on God every moment of every day.

One more warning – this book is rated PG-13. We don't have time to mince words when it comes to the crisis at hand. Now, let's get down to business. . .

INTRODUCTION

THE CULTURAL TSUNAMI

Do you remember the horrific Asian tsunami of December 2004 that wiped out parts of Indonesia and several other islands? There was another more recent tsunami that devastated Japan. The images from both tsunamis were unbelievable. The destructive power of the waves that moved through villages was nearly impossible for anyone in its path to survive. I will never forget those images. In Indonesia, people who were caught off-guard on beaches and in the fishing villages did not stand a chance against the power and force of the water that hit them and carried them away. One young woman survived by holding onto a tree, but she was one of the rare survivors of the direct impact.

The main reason that so many lives were lost, especially in Indonesia, was the absence or delay of any forewarning that a tsunami was coming. If people had foreknowledge, they would have had an opportunity to move to higher ground and be saved. Of course, there would have been those who refused to heed any warning since it was a beautiful, peaceful day on Indonesia's beaches right up until the tsunami hit. I'm sure, if warned, most people would have made some attempt to move to safety.

What if there had been a tsunami warning, but less dramatic language was used to describe the coming wave? What if the coming tsunami was described in the media as a large wave that MAY cause damage to the shoreline and had the POTENTIAL to be life-threatening, but the actual danger was downplayed? Even fewer people would take the warning seriously and run to safety. And what if the media for several years prior to this devastating event had portrayed a tsunami as a fun experience, showing video of people surfing and splashing around and laughing in a giant tsunami wave with little mention of the danger to human life? People would be much less likely to take deliberate, immediate action to move to safety in the face of a tsunami warning. Instead they would have gotten out their surf boards and beach balls and welcomed the coming wave.

I believe that the visual image of a tsunami is a powerful metaphor for the overwhelming wave of pressure that challenges an adolescent's identity and core belief system at about age 12, typically when they enter middle school. I call this phenomenon a *Cultural Tsunami*. This destructive wave of pressure comes through the school environment, television, movies, the internet, music, peers, older siblings and sometimes parents themselves. So often, adolescents don't know what hit them. Their entire perspective on their own identity and their relationship to the world around them is shaken to the core. Behavior that was once praised as good is now ridiculed. Beliefs about "good" and "bad" are turned upside down. Good is no longer good and bad is no longer bad. Clothing choices, hairstyles and body type that went largely unchallenged in elementary school are now looked down upon and harshly critiqued by peers.

Society has offered wishy-washy, half-hearted warnings that send mixed messages about the destructive nature of this *Cultural Tsunami*. Adolescents and teenagers are depicted on television and in movies having fun, splashing around in the waves of this *Cultural Tsunami* as they play around with sex and drugs with very mild, if any, negative repercussions. When consequences are depicted, they are typically softened to such a degree that any sense of reality is lost. The reality is that one in four teenage girls between the ages of 14 and

18 have, or have had, a sexually transmitted disease (STD).[8] Many of these STDs are untreatable and some cause infertility. One in six people in America (and one in five women ages 14-49) have genital herpes, which is incurable.[9]

Just today I heard Joseph Califano, Jr. interviewed on television. He was the Secretary of Health and Human Services from 1977 to 1979 and is currently the Chairman of the National Center on Addiction and Substance Abuse at Columbia University. He stated in the interview that children in America are typically very much against drug and alcohol use up through 5th grade. Children will even hound their parents to stop smoking and drinking. However, once they hit middle school and begin seeing peers smoking cigarettes or pot and drinking, their perspective begins to change. By the time children reach 8th or 9th grade, most are open to experimenting with drugs and alcohol themselves. The *Cultural Tsunami* has begun to carry them away.

We, as adults, play right into the hands of the *Cultural Tsunami* when we demonstrate an attitude of acceptance that this is just the way adolescents and teenagers are supposed to behave. We seem to have lost any sense of urgency when it comes to training our children to stand up against the tide. We hold our breath and hope for the best, then attempt to do damage control when we find ourselves in the middle of a crisis. We wonder what on Earth happened to our child.

Sexual innuendo on television, in movies and music begins to make sense around age 12 as peers at this age talk more openly about sexuality. Innocence is laughed at, so adolescents are pressured to adopt an edge to their personality and language to fit in and avoid embarrassment or humiliation. The worst possible label an adolescent can have is that of a "goody-goody." Kids who strived to do the right thing in elementary school and experienced praise and rewards in response, enter middle school to discover that they no longer have the luxury of just being themselves because the person they believed they were is no longer acceptable.

This *Cultural Tsunami* is a fact of life in America today. My question is, if we know a tsunami is coming why aren't we on high alert actively preparing our children? If we knew a real tsunami was coming when our kids hit age 12 and there was no way to avoid it, I feel certain we would all be spending hours each week in rigorous training with our children in the specific skills they would need to survive. In fact, a very real *Cultural Tsunami* is most certainly going to hit your child around age 12. It threatens to destroy, or at the very least damage them emotionally, psychologically and spiritually. It has the potential to change children permanently and sometimes render them drug addicts, alcoholics, or scarred by STD's and emotional damage for the rest of their lives. Why are we not more concerned? Why aren't more of us actively focused on preparing our children to stand against the *Cultural Tsunami*?

This *Cultural Tsunami* is damaging our young people in the deepest parts of their beings and is preventing them from becoming the magnificent adults that our society so desperately needs them to be. Instead so many of them reach adulthood wounded, bleeding, and in bondage emotionally, psychologically and spiritually. These deeply wounded young adults find it almost impossible to develop satisfying, long-term relationships with others. Therefore, the damage is passed from generation to generation. For many of them it takes a lifetime to heal from the wounds inflicted on them during the adolescent and teenage years, if they find healing at all. Another incredibly sad statistic about young adults today is that more than half of those who currently identify as being religiously unaffiliated have walked away from the faith they were raised in.[10]

My hope and prayer is that this book serves as a wake-up call. Each of us needs to begin in our own home with the people right in front of us to counteract the *Cultural Tsunami*. In his book entitled *High Society: How Substance Abuse Ravages America and What To Do About It*,[11] Califano makes the point that any person who reaches the age of 21 without smoking cigarettes, using illicit drugs or abusing alcohol is much more likely to never do those things in their lifetime. All the more reason to fight long and hard for our teenagers to come through this *Cultural Tsunami* victoriously!

If you do not have children or teenagers in your home, ask God to place adolescents and teenagers in your life that you can encourage, instruct and bless. If you have children or teenagers in your home, I hope to challenge and encourage you to parent boldly and with purpose. Prepare your children for the *Cultural Tsunami* that is to come. Boldly come alongside and join in the fight to save your teenager from drowning. God will be with you in the surging water!

SECTION ONE

THE DESTRUCTIVE NATURE OF THE CULTURAL TSUNAMI

CHAPTER 1

THIS IS WHY I WROTE THE BOOK

BOBBY'S STORY

Bobby was so relieved to have his junior year of high school behind him. It had been a stressful but rewarding year at the public high school he attended. He was also relieved to have the 'big decision' behind him regarding which full baseball scholarship he would accept. He had decided to stay close to home and go to the state university. Bobby was living a pretty typical, middle class American teenager's life. His parents were still married, which made him different than most of his friends whose parents were divorced and in many cases had remarried. His mom and dad both had good jobs and his little sister, Brianne, was less annoying than most little sisters.

Bobby had managed to stay away from the party scene that the vast majority of kids at his high school participated in. The athletes at his school were required to sign a contract forbidding them from drinking or doing drugs or even being at a party where others were drinking or doing drugs. Bobby had slipped up a couple times when he had a beer or smoked a joint with friends, but thankfully had not been caught. Still he felt left out on Mondays at lunchtime when his friends all talked and laughed about what they did when they were drunk or high over the weekend. They also talked about who had sex with whom. The girls were much more likely to do stuff when they were drunk or high. It all seemed like harmless fun and no one was getting hurt. Most of the kids crashed overnight at the party house so it was rare that someone would drive under the influence, except just to run up to the nearest convenience store. Most of the girls were on birth control, which made up for the unpredictable use of condoms when a guy was under the influence.

Bobby had a lot of free time on his hands this summer, which was unusual for him. Baseball camp was a month away and he was frustrated that his boss at the sporting goods store wasn't giving him many hours to work. His mom and dad worked until 6:00 p.m. most days and Brianne had a babysitting job for the summer. It was a Wednesday around noon when his best friend Kevin texted to see what Bobby was up to. Kevin and Bobby had lived in the same neighborhood and had been friends their whole lives. Bobby had slept in that morning and planned to play video games all afternoon. He wasn't scheduled to work that day, so hanging out at Kevin's sounded pretty good. Kevin told Bobby that he had invited Steven, a mutual friend, to come hang out with them.

When Bobby got to Kevin's house, Kevin and Steven had already lit up a joint. It was no big deal. No one would ever know. They offered Bobby a hit and he gladly joined in. It felt good to be participating in some of the fun his friends had been having. A rush came over him that was the best feeling he had experienced in a long time. No worries, life is good. He looked at his friends and thought about how lucky he was to have these two friends who had been with him through thick and thin. Then Steven got up and got something out of his backpack. He said it was a special joint. He assured Kevin and Bobby that it was the best weed ever and that it would give them the best high they had ever experienced. Bobby trusted his friends and knew they did this stuff all the time. He was ready to have the best high he had ever had. Didn't he deserve it after all the hard work he had done this past year?

It seemed like an eternity to Kevin as he tried to keep his friend calm while they waited for the ambulance to arrive. He had called 911 while Steven grabbed all the evidence and ran out the back door. Bobby was pacing around the room. He didn't seem to know where he was and thought people were coming to get him. He was seeing things that weren't there and hearing voices that Kevin didn't hear. His words were coming out all garbled and he was delirious. Kevin had never seen anything like this and had called 911 even after Steven had begged him not to. Kevin cared about his friend. The ambulance finally arrived.

When Kevin described the special joint Bobby had taken a couple hits off of, the paramedic figured it was 'wet' – marijuana soaked in embalming fluid then dried. Fortunately for Kevin, he had passed on it. The paramedics were seeing a lot of this, especially with teenage boys. Often the embalming fluid bought and used on the street had PCP and other chemicals in it as well. A police officer called Bobby's parents at work and told them to meet the ambulance at the local hospital.

Robert and Marge sped toward the hospital in stunned silence. Marge had remembered to call Brianne to tell her to stay overnight where she was babysitting. She protected her by saying that Bobby had just gotten sick and needed to be seen at the hospital but was going to be okay. The emergency room was overcrowded and chaotic. A nurse told Robert and Marge that Bobby was alive and had reacted badly to a drug he had taken. He was being seen by a doctor. She took them to a small waiting room. How could this have happened? There had to be some mistake! Bobby wasn't like the other kids at his high school. Bobby cared about his family, his life, and his future. He even sat with his family every Sunday at church. He was given the award for "good character" at the end-of-the-year assembly at school.

The doctor finally came in and told Robert and Marge that Bobby was stabilized. He described to them what Bobby had ingested and that his prognosis was uncertain. He explained to them that after a couple days of medical treatment, he would be transferred to the regional hospital, where he would be assessed and treated by a neurologist and a psychiatrist. A prognosis and treatment plan would be given at that time. Robert and Marge were escorted to an examination room to see their son, who was sleeping after an antipsychotic drug had been administered to sedate him.

The nurses at the regional hospital were very kind as they walked hurriedly from patient to patient. Sadness hung in the air as parents were coming and going to visit their adolescent and teenage children. Everyone seemed to walk with their heads down, avoiding eye contact. Bobby had a confused look when his parents walked into his room. It was as if he was saying, "I know I'm supposed to know you, but I don't remember." He wandered the halls and, in the common area he would pick up chairs and turn them over, as if he were attempting to make sense of his reality. He could speak, but his talk was simple and sometimes nonsensical. It wasn't any comfort to Robert and Marge to find out that there had been a dramatic increase in the number of teenage boys being admitted in various drug-induced states, many from smoking 'wet.' They were told on admission that within 10 days there would be a prognosis. Many of the boys being treated were able to regain most of their function, with only minor brain damage. However, some never did recover. All these parents could do, for 10 agonizing days, was hope and pray.

On day 11, they were scheduled to have a conference with the lead neurologist and psychiatrist treating Bobby. Robert and Marge thought they had seen progress so they remained hopeful that it would just be a matter of time before Bobby was back to normal and getting ready for his senior year of high school. Their hopes and lives were crushed when the doctors explained very slowly and methodically the damage that had been done to Bobby's brain and the grim prognosis. He did not show the signs of recovery they were looking for. He would not be able to return to a regular school and would, most likely, need assistance with basic living skills for the rest of his life. This family would never be the same.

LAURA'S STORY

Laura was considered a 'goody-goody' at her small public high school. Everyone knew everyone, and everyone in Laura's school had a reputation that was either good or bad. Laura was known for being very active in her church youth group. In fact, her social life almost exclusively revolved around her church. Laura didn't date, but had many boy friends. When she was a senior in high school, she and Jon seemed to be spending more and more time together until one day he asked her if she would go out with him. She surprised herself by saying yes. Laura and Jon had so much in common and had the same moral values. They were both virgins and both planned to remain virgins until their wedding night. As senior year drew to an end, Laura and Jon found themselves planning to go to different Christian colleges, about 2 hours apart. Jon gave Laura a ring that he said was a promise that they would eventually get engaged. He promised to visit her as often as he could once they got settled on their respective campuses.

The first few weekend visits were wonderful! Laura was so happy to see Jon and he seemed just as happy to see her. One weekend when Laura's roommate was away, they were sitting on the bed in Laura's dorm room. The door was cracked open a couple inches, as was the rule in the dormitory, but no one was around. They kissed more passionately than normal and Jon's hands wandered more than usual. Then Jon blurted out that he didn't see anything wrong with them having sex since they were committed to each other and were going to get married. He told Laura that he needed sex and couldn't go on like this. Laura gave in.

To Jon and Laura's relief, Laura didn't get pregnant. She decided to get on birth control right away and they found themselves having sex every time Jon visited. Then, one weekend, out of the blue, after having sex, Jon told Laura that he didn't feel the same way about her and was no longer sure that they were meant to be together for the rest of their lives. He was having doubts and was finding himself attracted to other girls on his campus. He told Laura that she could keep the ring he gave her, but that he wanted to break up. Laura was devastated.

Laura cried all weekend. She got herself together for her classes on Monday and her emotions settled into anger and bitterness. She had given Jon everything, only to be dumped! Word got around that Laura was now single. She started noticing guys looking at her differently. One guy in particular, Roger in her Psychology class, kept finding opportunities to start up conversations with her. She had always thought he was good looking, but never thought about him beyond that. Then one day he asked her out. She quickly accepted. Roger seemed like a really great guy. He was kind and considerate and professed to be a Christian. He told her that he had had sex before and didn't really think it was such a big deal. By their third date, Laura gave in. After that, their dates consisted of finding times and places they could have sex. Roger would then treat her to coffee or fast food. Some relationship! Laura began to feel dirty and used. She broke up with Roger. Neither one was heartbroken but Laura felt a sense a shame she had never felt before.

Laura decided to wait awhile before getting into another relationship. She regularly attended a small church near campus and tried to refocus on God. She had come to realize that she had begun to slip away from God. She was eager to get rid of the shame she felt and start fresh. She noticed a guy who looked to be in his early 20's named Dave who was always at church. He was sweet and shy, a little chubby and not what she considered good looking, but he wasn't ugly either. After some investigating, Laura found out that Dave had never had a girlfriend but was the nicest guy you would ever meet, and very committed to God. Laura was intrigued! One Sunday evening after church, Laura struck up a conversation with Dave and took the initiative to ask him out for coffee.

He accepted. After that, they began going out regularly after church services. Dave had his own apartment and eventually they went to his place to watch TV. Laura initiated some kissing and fondling, then she pushed it farther until Dave agreed to have sex.

Laura felt empowered being the one in control, the one doing the pressuring. The experience was rather awkward and not very satisfying for either of them, but Laura felt she could help Dave become more comfortable over time. After a couple more of these awkward physical sessions, Laura realized there was nothing fun about this. She also realized that she had nothing in common with Dave and didn't really even enjoy his company. Laura broke up with Dave. Dave was devastated. Laura was relieved but confused by her own behavior. The feelings of shame and guilt became stronger.

Finally, senior year in college had arrived. Laura was focused on graduation. She was a woman now with an exciting professional life ahead of her. She didn't need a man. She was rather proud of herself that she had only had three sexual partners in her four years of college. She tried to tell herself that she was still a good girl compared to other girls she knew. Most of her friends had had many sexual partners. She had learned to live with the ever-present feelings of shame and guilt. Then along came Derek.

Derek was also a senior and had big plans for his future as well. They had seen each other on campus over the years, but one of them always seemed to be in a relationship. Now they found themselves both single. Derek asked Laura out. On the first date, they had sex. Laura was a little surprised at herself allowing this to happen so quickly, but rationalized that it was love at first sight and maybe she had finally found the right person. Three weeks into their relationship, Laura woke up one morning in intense pain. The pain was coming from her groin area. She got up and went into the bathroom only to experience agonizing pain when she urinated. She let out a yell and her roommate came running. Something was very wrong! Laura asked her roommate to give her a mirror.

When she looked at her crotch, it was covered in large bumps and blisters.

Laura's roommate told her to get dressed and took her to the nurse's office on campus. The nurse took one look and told her that she had at least one sexually transmitted disease. She referred Laura to a gynecologist in town. The gynecologist diagnosed her with genital herpes, genital warts, and Chlamydia. The doctor gave her a prescription for the Chlamydia and a prescription to treat the outbreak, but explained that there is no cure for herpes or warts. He recommended she see a counselor on campus.

Laura was in so much pain she could barely walk. Her head was spinning as she was flooded with questions about who gave it to her and when, how unfair it was because she wasn't a slut, how was she going to tell her parents, and who would want to marry her now? Laura wanted to die!

After investigation, Laura discovered that it was Roger who infected her, even though he didn't have a visible outbreak at the time. She had proceeded to infect Dave then Derek, who broke up with her immediately.

WHAT CAN WE DO?

Both of these stories are based on real events and real people. Examples similar to these are unfortunately common occurrences in the lives of young people today. It used to be easy to tell the good kids from the bad kids and pot wasn't 'life threatening.' Parents who are basically good, caring, and involved can usually coast through the preschool and elementary school years without too much of a problem. We're able to navigate through the typical parenting challenges and appease our children when they are unhappy or when they challenge our authority.

Sometimes we even think it's cute when our young children challenge us. What's the harm when they're young and the stakes are not very high? The biggest problem we typically face in the early years of parenting is not having enough time in the day to complete all the tasks at hand. Kids sometimes whine too much or simply don't do what they are told.

For those parents whose children haven't yet reached adolescence, listen up! Take off your blinders and look around you. Your child is headed straight toward the *Cultural Tsunami* described in the Introduction. It typically hits at age 11 or 12, or about the time they enter middle school. The main purposes of this book are to wake you up to the need to prepare your pre-adolescent children to face this *Cultural Tsunami*, and to provide a lifeline for those of you whose teenagers are already being overwhelmed by the powerful waves of pressure.

Let's get down to business and dissect the teenage culture to give you a better understanding of what today's adolescents and teenagers are up against. Some of you may be shocked by the information presented in the next couple chapters while others of you already know first-hand what most teenagers face in their daily lives. There is no point sugar-coating the culture. We can sit in our comfortable homes wearing blinders while our kids are out on the front lines of the world, or we can wake up and get in the trenches with them.

The first section of this book will present a somewhat detailed description of the *Cultural Tsunami*. The second section will offer strategies, solutions, approaches, and per-spectives for parents to consider. Only the most courageous, bold, and mature parents will be up for the challenge. I hope that includes you! If you are smack dab in the middle of the *Cultural Tsunami* with your teenager, I will present effective ways to respond that you may not have considered.

I frequently have parents of teenagers respond to my suggestions with: "I've tried that already and it didn't work." You may have tried something a year or two ago, or even six months ago. Or you may have tried an approach briefly before going back to the status quo. When you apply a different approach to parenting, you must be consistent and stick with it. Children and teenagers are good at increasing the intensity of their behavior to get us to give up on a new approach and return to the status quo. I tell parents all the time to expect things to initially get worse when they change their approach. That's a sign that the new approach is working! Stick with it! You must mean business and outlast your child or teenager. Once again, courage, boldness, and maturity are prerequisites to applying these principles when parenting your teenager. The ultimate goal is for your child (and you) to be standing victorious when the waves die down on the other side of the *Cultural Tsunami*.

We're all together in this boat. I'm going to attempt to take us off of the Titanic and put us onto a cruise ship with a steady course mapped out ahead of us. We will most definitely hit a few waves on our cruise ship but we won't sink, and we will actually experience moments of joy on the journey. I hope you'll come along for the ride – our young people deserve to be rescued and set on the right course. After all, their personal future and the future of our culture rest in their hands!

CHAPTER 2

RESPECT FOR AUTHORITY (OR LACK THEREOF)

L et's start at the very beginning. It is my opinion that a lack of respect for authority is at the root of most of the struggles our teenagers are facing today. I also believe that the lack of respect for authority is a direct result of the behavior and attitudes of parents, especially in the early years of parenting. It's been my experience that many parents lack respect for authority figures in their own lives. (My detailed advice to parents on how to train (or re-train) children and teenagers to respect authority is described in the chapter entitled "The Brick Wall of Authority.")

The prevailing attitude of parents and children alike is often stated in the following ways: "You have to respect me first before I will respect you" or "I'm not giving you my respect unless you earn it." This sounds good on the surface, but the end result is most often disrespect in all directions. The fact of the matter is that to maintain a civilized society there must exist a basic respect for people in positions of authority, even before we know whether they deserve it or not. People in positions of authority such as teachers, police officers, parents, bosses, etc. must be granted respect based simply on their position before a word comes out of their mouths and even if they are imperfect.

The loss of this basic respect for positions of authority has resulted in teachers having to fight for the most basic respect sometimes for the entire school year. The simple fact that they are the teacher carries no weight with most students. Parents who themselves demonstrate this attitude toward authority figures find themselves having to fight for basic respect from their own children on a daily basis and often never receive it. If we require people to prove they are worthy of the most basic level of respect before we will grant it, we reserve the right to determine if and when they become worthy and more often than not we never grant respect. If we refuse to grant respect unless they first grant it to us, we again make ourselves the subjective judge of whether they ever deserve our respect, which typically never happens.

A good deal of my experience with teenagers currently takes place in the setting of the church. This is undoubtedly the place where I see the most respectful teenagers. However, the majority of teenagers I have encountered both in church and elsewhere become disrespectful the moment an adult attempts to place a restriction on their behavior or attempts to hold them accountable for their actions.

****

Disrespectful behavior takes many forms. It runs the gamut from attempts to coerce an adult into making an exception to a rule, to blatant, in-your-face defiance. The sweet young girl who attempts to weasel her way around the rules is being just as disrespectful of authority as the young man who gets in your face. That sweet-faced attempt at coercion can change to anger in an instant when the young lady is faced with an adult who holds steady and does not give in. When teenagers respond in an angry manner to adults who refuse to give in, it is because this isn't how the adults in their world typically respond to their requests or demands. It's like the teenager is saying "Hey, didn't you get the memo? This is the point where you give in and I get what I want!"

Patterns are developed during childhood and carry over into adulthood, unless a drastic shift along the way causes the young person to rethink their relationship to the world around them. Teachers see a response pattern in each and every student who walks into their classroom and can typically figure out, based on the student's response to their authority, how things work in the student's home life. Teenagers have developed a belief system about how they fit into the world based on their earliest experiences with their parents or caregivers.

By the age of five, children possess a well-developed core belief system about who they are in relation to the world and every subsequent experience in childhood either confirms or challenges this belief system.[12] Some children are in for a rude awakening when they walk through the door of their first classroom. The first day of school, kids bounce into the classroom with their cool new clothes and superhero book bags, ready to show the teacher and the other kids how the world works. Problems arise when the teacher and the other students do not respond in the way they expect. Many kids enter their first classroom believing they are the center of the universe. After all, they are the center of the universe in their own home. If an inexperienced or ineffective teacher has several kids in the classroom with this attitude (which is often the case), it will take weeks or months for the teacher to gain control of the classroom, if she ever does.

As children navigate their way through daycare and school, the core belief system that has been taught and reinforced daily by their parents regarding who they are in the context of the world around them either serves the child well or presents him with a myriad of challenges. If parents are overprotective and defensive of their child, the child continues to believe that they are the center of the universe and that the teacher who challenges them is pure evil or just plain stupid.

The child will not demonstrate respect for the teacher who is attempting to teach him to live among his peers in a cooperative manner if his parents don't demonstrate respect for authority figures in the child's life. This type of parent is often attempting to hold onto the loyalty of their child and sees teachers and other authority figures as a threat to their position in their child's life. In reality the child will develop little or no respect for the parent as well. The parent will experience this personal lack of respect the first time they attempt to stand up to their child or when the child gets big enough to get right back in their face.

****

A recent incident at a high school in our area clearly demonstrated the origins of lack of respect for authority. A young man was sent to the principal's office due to defiance demonstrated in the classroom. The principal called the young man's mother, who arrived at the school within minutes. This mother began screaming at the principal the minute she entered his office. The young man then picked up a stapler and threw it at the principal's head as the mother jumped on the principal's back and began beating him in the head and face. Both the student and the mother were subdued and arrested.

This was obviously an extreme situation, but that young man most certainly learned to disrespect and challenge authority from his mother. They were a regular tag team, going after any authority figure who challenged them. Once again, disrespectful behavior runs the gamut in how it is displayed. The same level of disrespect is often expressed verbally or symbolically rather than physically. In seemingly civilized homes all across America, children are very quietly being taught to disrespect authority figures in much more subtle ways.

A perfect example of a more civilized version of a mother teaching her son to disrespect authority was presented recently on the "Fox and Friends" morning show on the Fox News Channel. The seemingly newsworthy issue this particular mother and her five-year-old son described had to do with the length of the little boy's hair. The child's school had a policy that boys were to keep the length of their hair above the collar and this mother refused to cut her son's hair. There were no religious or cultural convictions involved in her decision. She just thought her son was cute with long hair and wasn't going to comply with the school's policy. As a result, the five-year-old was required by the school to receive instruction in the school library with a teacher's aide until the parents complied with this rule. The child and his mother were rewarded for their defiance with the sympathy and attention they received from the national media.

This is an obvious case of a parent not seeing the forest for the trees! This mother taught her child that standing up to authority figures is the goal regardless of the triviality of the issue. She missed an opportunity for a critical character-building lesson that had the potential to change the trajectory of her child's entire future. Again, there were no religious or cultural convictions that gave significance to the length of this child's hair. The mother and child simply preferred his hair longer.

This five-year-old most likely learned from the experience that no one at his school has a right to tell him to do anything he doesn't want to do for the next 12 years. Then beyond that, no boss or other authority figure has a right to tell him what to do or how to present himself. So there! We can only imagine where an attitude like that will take this precious little boy. This mother can be sure that the defiance she is instilling in her child will come back to bite her in the not-so-distant future. We see examples of the end result of this attitude in high schools and prisons all across the country.

Of course there are times to challenge the directives of authority figures. Challenges to authority, however, need to be reserved for issues of substance and need to be conducted in a way that instructs our children in appropriate, respectful ways to challenge authority. First there needs to be a foundation of respect for authority in the basic issues of life – even if it means cutting a couple of inches off of our child's hair during the school year just because the school requires it.

****

Every day in homes across America, well-meaning parents lovingly give in to their children to avoid upsetting them and to maintain peace and quiet in the home. Parents respond to incessant whining by allowing their child to stay up past their bedtime and fall asleep in front of the television, or by purchasing a needless toy off the shelf at Wal Mart. Parents talk the talk but don't walk the walk. Children are told over and over to brush their teeth and get ready for bed then nothing happens when the child ignores the parent and remains in front of the television. Children are allowed to argue with their parents with impunity. When a parent argues back and forth with their child, they are elevating the child to their level (or lowering themselves to the child's level). There is no distinction and no clear authority figure in that type of parent/child interaction.

Parents demonstrate patterns in their behavior which children quickly learn to read and expect. As a result, children develop patterns of responding to their parents' predictable behaviors. Thus goes the endless cycle of frustrated parents and disrespectful kids. Distraction is often the enemy of the parent. Parents yell instructions from another room and become frustrated when their child doesn't respond with obedience. We, as parents, spin our wheels and expend excessive amounts of energy then become angry and resentful because our mere, empty words mean nothing to our children. The same children grow up to become disobedient, disrespectful teenagers when the stakes are much higher and the behaviors more dangerous. Why would we expect our teenagers to demonstrate respectful, obedient behavior when we didn't require it of them in the smaller things when they were younger? And why would we expect our teenagers to demonstrate respect for us when we are constantly yelling and out of control. And, why do we expect our teenagers to demonstrate respect for us when we have taught them to disrespect other authority figures in their lives?

CHAPTER 3

SEX

As Christians, we can easily identify several Scriptural references that make it very clear that God takes sexual immorality of all kinds very seriously. In the Scriptures, the Apostle Paul urges us to "Flee from sexual immorality. All other sins a man commits are outside his body, but he who sins sexually sins against his own body."[13] The Scriptures do not say we are to try our best to avoid sexual immorality, Paul says we are to *flee* from sexual immorality. Sexual immorality affects us in a more profound way than other sins we may commit; therefore, the caution against sexual immorality in the Scriptures is clear and strong. It seems obvious that a loving God is attempting to protect us from consequences of sexual immorality, even when we are unaware of some of the potential consequences.

Some of you may remember when HIV and AIDS were unknown to us? I remember in the 1980's when the media began talking about this newly discovered sexually trans-mitted virus and we were warned that the average person could already have it and not know it. Also, the details of how it was transmitted were not yet fully understood. It was a very scary time. I find it hard to believe that there aren't even now unknown viruses being passed around and viruses in the process of mutating that will be just as deadly as AIDS was when it was first identified. Diseases continue to develop that attack us physically, and sex outside of the total commitment of marriage damages us on the deepest level of our being, often in ways only God can see.

****

God's not telling us to not have sex. After all, He's the one who created this amazing way to bond with another human being and make babies. He designed sex as the absolute, ultimate act of intimacy where we join together with another human being of the opposite sex in every possible way – physically, emotionally, spiritually and psychologically. Our entire being is involved to the point that we become one flesh with the other person. As it often is with other potential blessings, the world takes the beauty of sexual intimacy which God designed and twists it into something destructive, negative and/or meaningless.

God intended sex to be fun and pleasurable as well as having it serve the purpose of procreation. Then He told us that this ultimate act is a very big deal and is to be saved for the person to whom we commit our life. This command was not meant to ruin our fun, but to protect us and give us the gift of ultimate intimacy that He wants each of us to experience if we choose to marry. People who have had multiple sexual partners will often say that the more partners they had, the less special sex became, and the less special they felt to each partner. With multiple partners, the excitement is only there briefly with each new partner, then it becomes routine. Over time, sex becomes nothing special. A young man recently told a young woman in our church youth group that he is sexually active and that sex is really no big deal. His point was that saying no to casual sex is ridiculous and pointless, and that her commitment to sexual purity is silly. Her response to him was that she wants sexual intimacy to be a big deal between her and her future husband. This generation is being robbed of the specialness of sex in a marriage relationship. Their emotions and capacity for intimacy are being killed off deep within their beings and they don't even realize what they are losing. What a tragedy!

Another negative outcome from the increase in casual sexual behavior among young people is the decrease in young men who are interested in marriage. The sex drive is a powerful motivator. By condoning or accepting free and relatively unrestricted sex, we have taken away its power to motivate young people in positive ways and consequently have created a generation of young people experiencing the physical and emotional wounds that result from casual sexual behaviors. We have taken away the experience of commitment that makes sex and marriage special.

An intriguing article entitled "A Case Against Marriage" written by Jessica Bennett and Jesse Ellison appeared in the June 21, 2010 issue of *Newsweek* magazine. This article describes the thought processes of many twenty-somethings regarding relationships and marriage. The authors quote one 28-year-old young man as saying "If I had to be married to have sex, I would probably be married, as would every guy I know."[14] A recent television talk show addressed this issue. The host presented questions written by a panel of young adult women to a panel of young adult men. The first question the women wanted an answer to was "Why is it so difficult to get today's young adult men to commit to marriage?" The young men on the panel all smiled sheepishly then admitted that they can find a woman to have sex with whenever they want. Why then do they need to get married?

Think about the ripple effect that would occur in the lives of young people if more and more teenagers and young adults chose abstinence until marriage. More and more young people would choose to leave home, marry, and work hard to establish their own homes if it was the only way they would get sex and a warm body to sleep with at night. It always amazes me how many parents I talk to who have a single, adult son living in their home and will allow him to have young women spend the night or at least have conjugal visits in the home. At the same time he is being taken care of in every other way by mom and dad. The parents wonder why their son doesn't desire to get married and have his own home. Why would he be motivated to leave home or get married? This is the perfect example of someone having his cake and eating it too.

****

Among young adults who profess to be Christians there is still a belief that marriage is important; however, waiting to have sex until marriage is not considered to be a requirement these days. Of all the premarital counseling sessions I have conducted with Christian couples, approximately 90% of them were already living together. The following statistics were presented in the book *Living Together Myths, Risks and Answers* by Mike and Harriet McManus:

- Only two out of ten cohabiting couples are able to build a lasting marriage.
- Nearly half of cohabiting couples break up before the wedding.
- Those cohabiting couples who do marry are 50 percent more likely to divorce than those who had never lived together.[15]

The argument couples most often use to justify living together before marriage is that they want to ensure that they are compatible so that their marriage will be less likely to end in divorce. Statistics show just the opposite. As stated above, cohabitation actually increases the chances of the marriage ending in divorce.

In all the premarital counseling sessions I have conducted with young Christian couples who planned to marry in the church, I only encountered one young couple who were both virgins and were waiting until their wedding night to be sexually intimate. They didn't have sexual histories with other people that they had to work through as they approached marriage. Their pure, unjaded excitement as they anticipated that night was a beautiful thing! A few weeks after the wedding this new bride rushed up to me after church one Sunday to show me a wedding picture. When I asked her how everything was going, she knew what I was getting at and she smiled in response. It was a beautiful thing!

Now I think we Christians often built up the wedding night experience to a point that young people who do wait to be intimate often have such high expectations that the wedding night ends up being a letdown. As a result, they are disappointed in themselves and in the promise that if they waited, the result would be fireworks. Quite often, the sexual relationship takes time to develop into a mutually satisfying experience. The point is that by waiting until the wedding night, there is freedom to make the sexual relationship a truly beautiful, intimate experience without negative baggage getting in the way of intimacy.

I have had casual conversations with my own children's friends, teens at my church and in my practice that have absolutely blown my mind! These are not sheltered kids. A common belief that I hear expressed by young people is that they need to know ahead of time if they are sexually compatible before marrying someone and they don't want to be sexually inexperienced on their wedding night for fear of embarrassment. It makes no sense to me that a person would want to have that awkward first sexual experience with someone who doesn't even care about them as opposed to having that first experience with someone who loves and respects them enough to commit his or her life to them.

Teenagers and twenty-somethings seem so much more concerned about sexual compatibility in marriage than in emotional, psychological, and spiritual compatibility with their potential life partner. When asked about areas of incompatibility, the common response is that they believe they can work through or just accept other areas of concern or that their partner will change. Therefore, very little time is spent concentrating and working on emotional, psychological, and spiritual issues when deciding who to marry.

I guess we shouldn't be surprised to find that this generation of young people focuses on sexual compatibility as a top priority in a relationship given the overwhelming emphasis placed on sexuality in relationships in every form of media. Unfortunately, the emphasis in relationships is often placed on physical pleasure and the emotional high that comes along with it. Love is defined by the quality of the sexual experience.

As a result of this twisted, shallow thinking, young people often give away the most precious bonding experience a couple can have to an undeserving casual boyfriend or girlfriend, believing that the experience will actually help them to someday have a more satisfying wedding night. The reality is that by the time a young man or woman marries, they have typically been rejected more than once. They have typically given themselves away to insecure, immature, self-serving people who claim to care about them. In other words, they have been used and abused for someone else's sexual satisfaction more than once. How on Earth does this make for a more satisfying sexual experience in marriage? In addition, the sexual experience is no longer special and sometimes even has negative emotions attached to it because of past experiences. The reality is that having a sexual history makes sexual satisfaction in marriage more difficult to achieve. Disillusionment and resentment follow and marriages crumble. This is not the scenario God intended for romance and marriage.

****

The second most common belief about sex that teens seem to have internalized is that if you have a condom, you're good to go. They know that Sexually Transmitted Diseases (STD's) are something to fear but, once again, they believe that if they have a condom they're all set. Young women assume that every boy is born with the control and expertise to correctly use a condom in any given situation – even if alcohol is added to the equation. It's almost laughable if it wasn't so sad! If putting condoms in the hands of every teenager was the answer, there would be very few teenagers contracting STD's today.

****

We've all but lost the battle with media influence. Unless you're Amish, which looks pretty attractive these days, your kid will be exposed to sexually explicit images and information at a pretty young age. Don't make the mistake of assuming that The Disney Channel and Nickelodeon are always a safe choice. There was an episode of a popular program aimed at adolescents that depicted a scene where a teenage boy hid in a school janitor's closet with a teen girl he had a crush on. He came out of the closet with a stain on his pants. The stain was referenced and the boy responded in an embarrassed manner. Young children would not understand where the stain came from but all they have to do is ask an older sibling or friend to get an education.

Some of the Disney girls have been caught sexting (sending sexually explicit pictures over their cell phones or on the internet). Miley Cyrus and Vanessa Hutchens have turned out to be quite the little role models for their young audiences as pictures of them either half-naked or completely nude have appeared on the internet. As I'm writing this, there is an article in our local newspaper, "The York Daily Record", entitled "Sexting common among teenagers." The article cites a poll that found that "more than a quarter of young people have been involved in sexting in some form."[16] There have been situations where nude pictures of underage students were passed around schools in our local area. Most teenagers don't realize that this is considered to be the possession and distribution of child pornography under the law, which is a felony and often results in the person convicted being labeled a sex offender.

We should never give up closely monitoring the influences in our children's lives and restricting access to material we deem inappropriate. Our culture is so permeated with sexual content that it requires us to be that much more diligent in training our kids to live in the world but not of the world. Parents need to talk to their children about the celebrities they are looking up to and the choices these celebrities make. We must bring celebrities down to a human level and talk about them as though they are just like us, because they are. Call their decisions wrong and reckless when they are, but acknowledge how difficult it is to make decisions that go against the culture. When celebrities take positive stands, talk about that too.

****

Then there's the subject of pornography. Boys in our culture are almost guaranteed to be exposed to pornography online before they reach the age of 12. When one of our daughters was 8 or 9 years old, she asked if she could use my screen name and password to access Google. We had put all kinds of restrictions on the computer that our kids used in an attempt to protect them from unintentional (or intentional) exposure to sexual images. Our daughter was researching Japanese rope bridges for a paper she was writing for social studies class. This specific research seemed completely harmless so I allowed her the access. Before long I heard a scream and loud footsteps coming down the stairs. Into the kitchen she came, looking horrified and yelling "I hate when that happens!" She had clicked on a site that looked informational and suddenly, before her eyes, was an image of naked Japanese people engaged in sexual activities involving ropes! Who'd have thought??? Her response was to immediately click out of the site.

That story is a perfect example of what frequently happens in the lives of young boys. The difference is that young boys don't typically scream and run to their mothers. More often, their sexual curiosity is peaked and they take it all in. That initial exposure opens a door that typically remains open for years to come. Each exposure increases the desire to see more and on and on it goes.

On the subject of pornography, the culture says, "What's the big deal? They're just pictures. It's part of the learning process." The truth is it is a big deal. Those pictures, introduced into the minds of pre-adolescent and adolescent boys, create perceptions and beliefs that forever influence their impressions of women and sexuality. I don't want to get too graphic, but adolescent boys quite often have their first sexual experiences with the women in the pornographic pictures. Their minds fill in the blanks. Those women are often portrayed as submissive, sexual beings whose only desire is to give themselves to these young men. Yes, it's just a fantasy but the immature mind of an adolescent or teenager processes it as though it's reality. The women in the pictures don't have personalities, except for what the young man gives them in his fantasy. These women don't have personal preferences or opinions. They make no demands and are only focused on giving pleasure. By the time a young man, who has saturated his mind with pornographic images and fantasies of women, is ready to have a real relationship with a real woman, his mind has been warped to the point that he doesn't see real women as complex human beings who deserve to be respected. He is looking for the fantasy woman from the pictures because that's who he is already emotionally and psychologically bonded with. No real woman can possibly measure up.

I have been told by adult men who struggle with pornography addiction that they believed that as soon as they got married the addiction would resolve on its own. They found out otherwise. The addiction often gets worse because their wives have minds of their own. Sex is never quite fulfilling because real live women are complex. Wives have emotional needs as well as personalities, opinions, and expectations. Even if wives tell their husbands everything they want to hear, husbands know that there's an emotional component to intimacy with their wives. If they have been viewing porn for any length of time, they have experienced sexual pleasure hundreds of times with no emotional connection involved.

Fantasy women don't have emotional needs so once the sexual encounter is over, the woman is gone with the click of a mouse - no emotional expectations or needs to worry about or try to meet. Fantasy women are always in awe of a man's sexual prowess so the man has nothing to prove. He can never be judged or critiqued. There are no expectations to live up to in fantasy world and the man is completely and totally in control of the sexual experience, beginning to end. For these reasons, men often report that the combination of self-gratification and pornography is more satisfying than sex with their wives. Once again, husbands and wives are robbed of the amazing, fulfilling experience of intimacy that God intended, and it typically starts with that first exposure to pornography as an adolescent.

Feminist author Naomi Wolf recently published an article entitled "Is Porn Driving Men Crazy?" In this article, she cites research that demonstrates how pornography desensitizes men sexually. As a result, these men "required higher levels of stimulation to achieve the same level of arousal."[17] Wolf states that:

> "The experts I interviewed at the time were speculating that porn use was desensitizing healthy young men to the erotic appeal of their own partners."[18]

She also speaks to the addictive potential of pornography, citing research which shows that:

> "porn delivers rewards to the male brain in the form of a short-term dopamine boost, which, for an hour or two afterwards, lifts men's mood and makes them feel good in general. The neural circuitry is identical to that for other addictive triggers, such as gambling or cocaine."[19]

Wolf's analysis demonstrates that the secular world is beginning to realize the destructive power of pornography over individuals and relationships. We must do everything in our power as parents to protect our children and teens from exposure to pornography. We also must deal with our own pornography use and face the fact that if we are viewing pornographic images ourselves, we must confess our sin, repent, and seek help to break this bondage in our own lives. If you think your teenager doesn't know that you view pornography, you're most likely wrong. In most cases, they know.

****

The latest information I am hearing from teenagers is that many of them are not having traditional intercourse. Girls believe that they can still call themselves virgins if they haven't had sex the traditional way. They will do everything else but have traditional sex. The girls I work with often tell me that guys don't seem to care what form the sexual encounter takes. This is further evidence of the teenage mindset that I spoke of in the introduction. A restriction is something to get around. If traditional sex is too risky and girls are hesitant out of fear of possible consequences or the desire to technically remain a virgin, don't let that stop you - find another way. This is also a direct result of ideas and desires planted in the minds of young men through pornography. Another recent trend is dating in threesomes – usually two girls and one guy. Based on my experience counseling and working with teenagers, it seems that alternate forms of sexual activity are becoming increasingly accepted.

As Christians, we seem to struggle with our response to homosexuality, bisexuality, and alternate forms of sexual activity. The Bible is clear that anything outside of one male and one female within marriage is sexual immorality. All a Christian has to read to understand God's intentions regarding sexuality is the creation account in Genesis. God originally created us to pair up as one male and one female. Behavior outside of that original design began to occur after Adam and Eve rebelled. If you wish to explore the biblical view of homosexuality, I recommend the book *A Biblical Point of View on Homosexuality* by Kerby Anderson.[20] Mr. Anderson provides a respectful, clear, and well-documented explanation of what the Bible says on the subject.

I believe we, as Christians, struggle with responding to alternative sexual choices because the culture has successfully demonized those who call sexual immorality a sin. If we take a stand against the normalization of alternative sexual practices, we are called bigots and haters. If we were truly bigots and haters, we would not recoil from such labels. True Christians devoted to Christ understand the emphasis that Jesus places on love for all of His creation and the last thing we want to demonstrate in our lives is bigotry and hatred. However, the tension occurs when love is defined by the culture as the acceptance of a variety of sexual choices as moral equivalents. Any response that is not totally accepting is labeled 'hate'.

Some people do seem to be strongly tempted by same sex attraction, often from a very young age, when others are not. We all have our particular, unique struggles and there are a myriad of theories that attempt to explain sexual attraction. I do agree with many in our culture who believe that we do not necessarily choose to be attracted to the same sex or opposite sex or both. However, our temptations are not our identity. Therefore, I strongly believe that being tempted by same-sex attraction does not make the person homosexual. Hebrews 4:15 says that Jesus "was tempted in every way, just as we are, yet was without sin."[21] Jesus has experienced what it's like to be tempted by sexual desires. Again, I believe that just because a person is tempted to engage in homosexual behaviors does not make them a homosexual by identity. Only when a person gives themselves over to the homosexual lifestyle does it become their identity, by their own choice. James 1:13-15 describes very clearly the progression from temptation to sin to death. Each step of the way we have a choice to make.

> "When tempted, no one should say, "God is tempting me." For God cannot be tempted by evil, nor does he tempt anyone; but each one is tempted when, by his own evil desire, he is dragged away and enticed. Then, after desire has conceived, it gives birth to sin; and sin, when it is full-grown, gives birth to death." [22]

If abstinence is the only way to stay sexually pure, so be it. We are not animals who have no control over our flesh. Our bodies may want to do many things and the desire may be very strong; however, we still have the ability to reason and decide if we are going to say yes or no to these physical desires.

****

Recently I saw a woman on television being interviewed from prison. I remembered this woman from the intense media interest in her criminal trial a few years ago. She was a high school teacher found guilty as an accessory to the murder of her husband, who was murdered by her high-school-student/lover. This woman's final comment in the interview was: "I wish I had listened to my brain instead of my body. I knew what I was doing was wrong. If I had listened to my brain none of this would have happened and my husband would still be alive." This woman learned a profound lesson in a very tragic way. We need to teach our children to listen to and follow what their brain knows to be right in situations where their body is demanding something that they know is wrong.

We treat sex as though it is a drive that we have absolutely no power over and must act upon. We treat teenagers as though they are wild animals who have no ability to control their response to their sexual urges. Children and teenagers who experience sexual attraction to people of the same gender are taught by the culture that this attraction makes them homosexual and that they have no choice but to accept it and hook up with a person of the same gender. Boys who exhibit less masculine characteristics are often labeled "gay" by their peers as early as elementary school. They are made to feel that they have absolutely no choice in the matter, so they may as well give themselves over to the homosexual life-style. They are also told that they will never be happy unless they give themselves over to their sexual urges.

We don't choose the particular areas of temptation that we are most challenged by and we all have powerful areas of personal struggle. I Corinthians 10:13 is a very well-known passage in the Bible. It says: "No temptation has seized you except what is common to man. And God is faithful; He will not let you be tempted beyond what you can bear. But when you are tempted, He will also provide a way out so that you can stand up under it."[23] This applies to temptation of every kind. God doesn't say He will remove the temptation, but He promises that He will provide a way out. It's up to us in those moments to look for the way out and choose to take it. Determination and action is required on our part to resist the temptation before it results in sin. Remember the Scripture I mentioned earlier that commands us to "flee from sexual immorality?"[24] If it's more than you can resist, FLEE! It's that important!

We are putting the cart before the horse when we refuse to physically remove ourselves and stop engaging in particular behaviors that we know are sinful while praying and waiting for God to zap us and remove the temptation. Once again, we behave as though we are helpless victims of our body's desires and must engage in whatever behaviors our body demands. As a culture, we pass that expectation along to our children and teens.

A perfect example of this mentality is a young man I went to church with when I was growing up. He said that he had cried out to God to remove his homosexual desires and that God didn't remove the desire. He blamed God for the homo-sexual lifestyle he was living. He remained in the lifestyle as he continued to beg and plead and blame God for not taking away the temptation and the desire. My questions in response to my friend were, "Did you look for the way out that God provided to make it possible for you to stand up under the temptation and not give in to sin? Did you flee, and literally leave the environment you were living in to do your part in removing yourself from temptation? Did you determine that you were going to live a life obedient to Christ no matter what sacrifice your flesh had to endure?" Perhaps sometimes we don't really *want* to be delivered.

****

One evening in the small group of teenage girls I was leading, we were talking about sex. They are often interested in hearing a different perspective from what they hear every other day of the week. I asked, point blank, how many of them were sexually active. Half of them were bold enough to raise their hands. I began talking to them about the risks they were taking when the one girl blurted out "I'm gay." I had heard rumors about this but hadn't given it much thought. The girl sitting next to her automatically leaned over in a very con- descending manner like she was speaking to a small child and said "It's okay. There's nothing wrong with it." I gently responded "Yes, homosexual behavior is sexual immorality the same as what some of the rest of you are doing. It's no worse but it's equally sin."

This girl and I had a straightforward, respectful discussion after everyone else left. I told her that I didn't think any differ- ently about her knowing this, but I cautioned her about sexual immorality just like the girls involved in heterosexual immo- rality. I explained to her that it was not a foregone conclusion that homosexuality was her identity, but that it was up to her to choose or reject the lifestyle and the behavior. She was still just as welcomed into our church group as she always had been, but some of the other girls were angry with me for saying what I did because they said I was being judgmental.

The judgmentalism Jesus condemned referred to our own personal judgment of others that comes out of a critical, arrogant spirit. When we identify a behavior as sin based on Scripture, the Scriptures are making the judgment and we are referring to the conduct, not the person. We must respect our teens enough to tell them the truth and still treat them with love and respect. What they do with that truth is up to them.

****

There is a seemingly small percentage of mature Christians setting an example of sexual purity and self-discipline for this upcoming generation. This generation of young people is in desperate need of role models who actually live up to the values they profess. Many adult women are struggling to find a sense of their own value as human beings. This generation of adult women and those before them have contributed greatly to society and I believe that there have been positive contributions made by the women who have broken through the societal barriers that existed prior to the feminist movement. However, I have seen many societally accomplished mothers who are still struggling with deep insecurities about their own purpose, value and worth.

The majority of the women I encounter, both professionally and socially, are profoundly disappointed and unhappy with the state of their personal lives and relationships. Accomplishments in the workplace will never replace the fulfillment and satisfaction of creating and maintaining a loving, stable family life. Men in our culture are often confused about their role in the family. Our culture has challenged their masculinity often to the point of marginalizing them and neutralizing their positive influence on the next generation. How can young people aspire to fulfilling, mature Christian lives and relationships if all they see around them in the church and the world are adults devastated by divorce, addictions and unfulfilling relationships?

Teenage girls today seem to be more insecure than ever and are giving themselves and their futures away often for the pleasure of teenage boys. Teenage girls are often vulnerable to the sweet talk, sexual advances and subsequent rejection of boys. Some teenage girls seem desperate for the attention of boys and will give almost anything to get it. That attention makes them feel special in the moment. Of course, the absence of fathers in our culture of divorce contributes greatly to this desperation. Could it also be that these young women are being raised by a generation of women who are themselves desperately searching for that same sense of personal value and significance?

****

Teenagers, and the culture at large, have come to the conclusion that it's almost impossible, and really too much to ask, for teenagers and adults alike to demonstrate sexual restraint. As a result of this attitude, girls who don't believe that any man will ever love them enough to commit his life to them and never leave (especially if Daddy didn't), will settle for whatever feels like love. Young men are settling too. They have no idea how great sex can be if saved for marriage and unfortunately most of them will never experience the level of sexual fulfillment that is possible in a committed relationship where true love is practiced. The current approach to sex is typically - use a condom, be somewhat choosy, and then go for it.

Sexual temptation is one of the strongest temptations we all face. Sexual immorality is sexual immorality, whether it is heterosexual, homosexual or bisexual. I'm no better of a person because my sexual desires are heterosexual. Inappropriate heterosexual temptation is just as important to resist as homosexual temptation. The overriding problem in our culture is that we treat all sexual desire as though we must satisfy it. We bow down to it and sometimes sacrifice our very lives and families to it. Doesn't that sound like idol worship?

It's as though saying no to our flesh is too much to ask of us as 'mere humans.' Most of us have no idea the peace, joy, intimacy and deep fulfillment we are missing out on by settling for the cheap, immediate substitutes that sin offers.

In Chapter 8 I talk about how Joseph in the Old Testament ran out in the street naked to keep from giving in to sexual temptation. He ended up unfairly jailed as a result, but that didn't change his resolve to remain obedient to God. Tremendous blessings followed as a result of Joseph's unwavering obedience to God.[25] Many of us have lost the will to say no to our flesh and have become complacent about sin. We often look for loopholes or rationalizations in Scripture rather than following the directive to "abstain from the appearance of evil."[26] As Christians, especially in America, pleasure and comfort has often become a higher priority than obedience to God and sacrifice in the name of Christ. Are we going to continue looking the other way, merely throwing out suggestions to our children hoping that they don't end up too damaged as they figure out sexual boundaries on their own or will we boldly step up, admit our own shortcomings, and get in the battle? Your children desperately need you in the battle with them!

WHAT CAN WE DO?

We must take our children's exposure to sexual content and opportunities for sexual temptation very seriously and partner with our kids in a very intentional way to do everything in our power to help them stay sexually pure in mind, body and spirit. As they are growing up, we must put as many roadblocks between them and sexual content as we can, even if it means they watch limited or no television and have extremely restricted access to the internet. We must very carefully monitor who they spend time with and require that their bedroom door stays open any time another child is in the room with them. Teenagers of the opposite sex should never be allowed in a bedroom together, even if the door is cracked open.

If you set clear, immovable boundaries from the beginning, you will have less conflict when hormones are raging. All of this can be done in a way that does not feel oppressive to the child. We must not instill in our children fear or anxiety about their sexuality. However, we can establish habits and rules that are presented as routine and we can be vigilant in monitoring our children without them even realizing just how vigilant we are!

We must educate our children on healthy, appropriate sexuality and answer any and all questions they have, without over-reacting or appearing disgusted or shocked by their questions. It is so important that we become our child's primary resource on questions about sexuality and that we influence our child's earliest impressions of sexuality. We must instill in our children, without reservation, the values that we hold. They need to hear from us very clear, confident messages of right and wrong and that these are not subjective judgments we came up with, but are clearly stated in Scripture. It is also important that our children learn that God established rules and boundaries to protect us because He loves us. Talk to your child about the negative consequences of sexual activity outside of marriage and let them know what the expectations are in your home before they have a serious boyfriend or girlfriend.

When your children are old enough to want to spend time with someone of the opposite sex, thou shalt not freak out! Allowing a friend of the opposite sex to accompany the family on an outing or come over to hang out with the family is appropriate. However, there must not be time alone in any room of the house. I heard of a situation where parents found out, after the fact, that their teen had a sexual encounter in the family room under a blanket while the rest of the family was in another part of the house.

Adolescents or teens will often make a huge fuss about any restrictions their parents impose regarding the opposite sex. Their hormones are screaming at them that they want opportunities to get physically close even if they have no intention of going all the way. They will ridicule their parents, promise their parents that they aren't going to do anything inappropriate and accuse their parents of embarrassing them or not trusting them. As parents, it is so important to stand firm and confident and not waiver! If your adolescent or teen loses a boyfriend or girlfriend or suffers ridicule from their peers, it's a small price to pay for maintaining their purity! Remember, it is better to err on the side of being too strict than to back off and be wishy-washy with your teen. You can always re-think your rules and adjust them the next time if you come to the conclusion that you were overly strict in a situation.

If you discover that your teen is already sexually active, you must intervene in a decisive way. As long as they are living under your roof, you have every right and responsibility to set limits on what happens in your home. Pray about it, discuss the situation together as parents and with your teen, and take whatever action you need to in an effort to remove the opportunity for sexual activity. If your child is a girl, take her to a gynecologist and have her checked for STD's and possible pregnancy. If your child is a boy, take him to the pediatrician or family doctor and have him checked for STD's. Your teen must realize the serious risk they are taking when they are sexually active and the responsibility that comes along with it. If the relationship is a serious one, place restrictions on when and where the couple is allowed to be together. Include their boyfriend or girlfriend in the discussions about expectations. You will possibly have an angry son or daughter on your hands and much screaming, crying and/or threatening may ensue, but you must stay calm, confident and decisive. You must be clear that there will be no sexual immorality practiced in your home. (I offer further guidance on achieving these goals in the second section of this book.)

Having a church family and youth group leaders affirming you and your goals as a parent is critical since the world is telling your teen the exact opposite. This is a hard sell if you are a single parent who has someone of the opposite sex sleeping over or living with you! Don't expect that your teen will respect any limits you place on their sexual activity if you are engaging in sexual immorality yourself. When it comes to sex, you are the only one between your child and the sexual tsunami that desires to drag them away!

CHAPTER 4

DRUGS

T his is a subject I wish to God I didn't have to know about or discuss. Alcohol and drugs (often prescription drugs) are destroying many young people in this generation. Through my experience with young people, I have come to believe that marijuana possibly poses the single largest threat to this generation. For this reason, most of this chapter specifically addresses pot smoking. However, the approach presented for addressing drug and alcohol use can be applied regardless of the substance your child is abusing.

If you're not concerned about the growing acceptance of marijuana in our culture, you should be. I have been shocked to find that only a handful of teenagers I have encountered in recent years believe that there is anything wrong with or dangerous about smoking pot. Their only concern is that it is illegal and the consequences they may face if they are caught with marijuana. The handful that I found who were concerned about marijuana was most likely comprised of compliant kids just telling me what they thought I wanted to hear.

The common rationalization I hear from today's teenagers is that alcohol and cigarettes are more dangerous and addictive than marijuana and they're legal. Yes, we are to respect and live within the law, but that doesn't mean that everything that is legal is necessarily good for us. From Christian kids I hear the rationalization that marijuana is just a plant and if God didn't intend us to use it He wouldn't have put it on the Earth. My response is that the same could be said of many plants and substances including arsenic, hemlock and tobacco, which are obviously dangerous to humans when ingested. Many animals that are part of God's creation are dangerous to humans and would not be a logical choice to have as household pets. At the time of creation, these plants and animals may not have been harmful to humans. However, we know that nowadays there are many elements of creation that are dangerous and sometimes lethal to humans. God gave us a brain to figure out what to ingest and what to avoid, and which animals to keep as pets and which animals to approach with caution. He tells us throughout Scripture to be discerning of good and evil in our decision making.

God desires for us to live in a way that allows us to achieve His full potential and plan for our lives. We know from Scripture that His plan is a good plan that gives us hope and a future.[27] In reference to His followers, Jesus says: "I have come that they may have life, and have it to the full."[28] That is His desire and plan for us. Drugs and alcohol have the potential to steal our lives and completely destroy us. At the very least, drugs and alcohol derail or sidetrack us from God's perfect plan.

****

Our culture has been very effective at getting across the message regarding the dangers of tobacco usage. As I'm writing this, the Food and Drug Administration (FDA) has introduced a new, more graphic warning label that is required to be printed on every pack of cigarettes in hopes that it will deter more people from smoking. Once a society decides to vilify a behavior or substance, it only takes one generation to turn around the perception of that behavior or substance. Of course, there are still adults and teenagers who smoke cigarettes, but the health dangers associated with cigarette smoking are accepted by our culture. The opposite seems to be true in our culture regarding the use of marijuana. Those in positions of power and influence seem ambivalent about it. At the current time it seems that the tide of public opinion is moving in the direction of legalizing marijuana in America.

Many of the adults in positions of power today grew up in the 60's when the youth culture was all about experimentation with drugs and sex. This fact could possibly explain some of the seemingly mixed messages we hear from our leaders regarding marijuana. Interestingly enough, an article came out in the past couple days announcing that Paul McCartney, at age 69, has given up his lifelong pot smoking habit. McCartney told *Rolling Stone Magazine* that "When you're bringing up a youngster, your sense of responsibility does kick in, if you're lucky at some point."[29] McCartney has an 8-year-old daughter and he apparently has come to the conclusion that being a pot-smoking Dad isn't the best parenting decision. If pot is harmless and funny, why would he believe that his use of pot would be irresponsible behavior as a parent?

I have been shocked by the number of adults in my own generation who admit to being regular pot smokers since they were teenagers. One woman brought her 12-year-old son in to see me because he was extremely disobedient and angry. She couldn't figure out what his problem was. She expressed that she was unaware of any reason for his anger. When she left the room and I began to talk to him, he blurted out "Look, I know where her marijuana stash is hidden under the pipes in the cabinet under her bathroom sink. When she gets stressed, she closes her bedroom door and smokes. Who does she think she is telling me to turn off my video games when she's a pothead?" Potheads are absolutely clueless about how their habit is affecting those closest to them. When this mother and I openly discussed the fact that her son knew exactly what she was doing, she seemed genuinely shocked. She really believed that she had successfully hidden her habit from her son and that her habit had no negative impact on him. In fact, she believed that pot smoking made her a better mother! Clueless!

****

The National Institute on Drug Abuse put out a fact sheet on marijuana that clearly explains the dangers of using this drug. This fact sheet states the following:

"In fact, marijuana smoke contains 50 to 70 percent more carcinogenic hydrocarbons than does tobacco smoke. It also induces high levels of an enzyme that converts certain hydrocarbons into their carcinogenic form – levels that may accelerate the changes that ultimately produce malignant cells. Marijuana users usually inhale more deeply and hold their breath longer than tobacco smokers do, which increases the lungs' exposure to carcinogenic smoke. These facts suggest that, puff for puff, smoking marijuana may be more harmful to the lungs than smoking tobacco."[30]

Pot is insidious and subtle in the way it changes a person. The use of marijuana could actually be considered more dangerous than tobacco use due to its effect on cognitive skills and social behavior. This same NIDA fact sheet explains these effects:

"Research clearly demonstrates that marijuana has the potential to cause problems in daily life or make a person's existing problems worse. Depression, anxiety, and personality disturbances have been associated with chronic marijuana use. Because marijuana compromises the ability to learn and remember information, the more a person uses marijuana the more he or she is likely to fall behind in accumulating intellectual, job, or social skills. Moreover, research has shown that marijuana's adverse impact on memory and learning can last for days or weeks after the acute effects of the drug wear off."[31]

Another misconception people have is that marijuana is not addictive. It may not be addictive in the same way that cigarettes, alcohol and heroin are addictive, but it is addictive nonetheless. According to the NIDA:

"Drug craving and withdrawal symptoms can make it hard for long-term marijuana smokers to stop abusing the drug. People trying to quit report irritability, sleeplessness, and anxiety. They also display increased aggression on psychological tests, peaking approximately one week after the last use of the drug."[32]

****

A young man who was a daily user of marijuana for 10 years recently described to me some revelations he has had about himself since he stopped smoking pot several months ago. Under the influence of marijuana, he had lost interest in daily hygiene, re-wore dirty clothes, stayed in a dead-end job that required very little of him even though he has a college degree, didn't notice or care if his apartment was clean or not and thought everything was just fine! When family members tried to bring these problems to his attention, he became defensive and thought to himself that everyone else had anger issues and needed to chill. Now that his head is clearing, he has realized that his teeth were becoming disgusting due to lack of regular oral hygiene, he (and his apartment) smelled disgusting, and he began to notice the reactions he was getting from people in social situations. Under the daily cloud of marijuana use, he just didn't care about much of anything and thought everyone else had issues, not him. He now realizes that his own choices were creating most of his problems. Without the effects of marijuana, he has come face to face with some difficult situations and emotions that he had avoided for years. He has some catching up to do in the area of emotional maturity. He actually resorted to alcohol use as a substitute for marijuana for a period of time, but made the decision to refrain from all substance abuse and is facing life head on (with a lot of help). He's learning that life can be hard, but that a healthy life and healthy relationships are so worth the struggle!

****

Did you know that we all have a running dialogue in our heads? Some people in my profession call it "self-talk" and it holds a powerful influence over an individual's emotions, sense of self and decision-making processes. A person who constantly repeats in their head the message that they are worthless, for example, will behave according to that message. If that same person changes the dialogue in their head to messages affirming personal value and worth, their core beliefs and behavior will also change over time. Those from my generation will remember the humorous Daily Affirmations by Stuart Smalley on *Saturday Night Live*. Stuart Smalley would look in the mirror every day and say "I'm good enough. I'm smart enough. And doggone it, people like me."[33] In all seriousness, therapists and psychologists understand the power of the messages we tell ourselves in our heads and often focus on this very powerful instrument of change when helping their clients.

The use of marijuana specifically, as well as other drugs, changes the dialogue in a person's head. Rarely, if ever, does the marijuana user take responsibility for himself or the pain his behavior is causing others. Pot tells him that, no matter what is going on in his life, he is not the problem. Someone else is to blame. No wonder people love this drug so much! Taking responsibility is painful and pot has told them the lie that they are the innocent victim, even if their entire family is yelling at them - especially if their entire family is yelling at them. So, if nothing is ever their fault then there is no need for them to grow and change as an individual.

Maturity comes when a person faces challenges head on and perseveres. James 1:4 says: "Perseverance must finish its work so that you may be mature and complete, not lacking anything."[34] One of the main reasons people smoke marijuana is to avoid fully experiencing the challenges of life, which often include uncomfortable or painful feelings and situations. The pot smoker isn't into the whole perseverance thing. The attitude is, "I'm chill. Why can't everyone else just be chill?"

****

God addresses the power of self-talk in Scripture with verses about the importance of a person's thought life. When the Psalmist talks about meditating on the Word, day and night[35], he is indicating an understanding of the power of his own thoughts and the messages he dwells on day and night. He chose to actively train his mind to focus on Scripture. The Apostle Paul clearly instructs us concerning our thoughts in Philippians 4:8. He says:

"whatever is true, whatever is noble, whatever is right, whatever is pure, whatever is lovely, whatever is admirable – if anything is excellent or praiseworthy – think about such things."[36]

Paul tells Christians to aggressively take control of their thought processes in 2 Corinthians 10:5 when he says: ". . . we take captive every thought to make it obedient to Christ."[37]

When a person uses mind-altering drugs, they put their thought life under the influence of the drug and open their mind to be influenced by just about anything or anyone who comes along. Alcohol, illicit drugs and some prescription drugs disable the gatekeeper of the brain and allow any voice to come in and take up residence.

Adolescence is typically fraught with self-doubt, insecurities, confusion and questions about self-worth. Adolescents are actively looking for answers that ease their doubts, answer their questions, and offer a positive sense of self. Feelings are the guiding force in the lives of immature adolescents. When teenagers get a taste of the phony quick fix for negative feelings that is marijuana, they become hooked psychologically and emotionally and fall in love with it. Marijuana is a counterfeit substitute for the authentic answer to all of their doubts and fears – a relationship with God and an understanding of who God created them to be in this world. We need to reach these kids before marijuana does, because once this deceiver has taken up residence in their minds and hearts and is influencing their thoughts, breaking that bondage can be extremely difficult.

****

I was watching television one day when a Christian program came on featuring a guest speaker named Dr. Richard Marks of Mastering Life Ministries.[38] I had never heard of this gentleman or his ministry, but I was immediately intrigued by what he was saying about addictions. I grabbed a pen and pad of paper and began taking notes. He spoke of how pain pursues pleasure. There is no truer statement than that. It is true physically, psychologically and emotionally.

When we are in emotional pain, we seek relief from that pain. Whether as a result of social pressures, family situations, or both, the typical adolescent experiences deep emotional pain often on a daily basis. I see many such adolescents in my office. This emotional pain makes them extremely vulnerable to anything that offers immediate relief and reassurance, and gives them pleasure in return. The reason so many adolescents turn to immediate pleasure is that they have not yet developed the maturity or the skills to persevere through pain or to stand alone against the culture. The easy availability of alcohol, marijuana and willing sexual partners requires adolescents today to be even stronger than was required of my generation if they are going to stand against these temptations.

Once an adolescent experiences the positive emotional and psychological effects of marijuana and alcohol, they often bond with those substances and soon a pathological relationship is developed between the person and the drug. The more they bond with the drug, the more they pull away from people. After all, people have caused their pain. Pot becomes their best friend. Parents almost always report noticing a significant difference in their relationship with their child that coincides with the child's introduction to marijuana.

Because of the psychological and emotional relationship that is developed between the user and their marijuana, users become very defensive when you criticize their 'best friend?' It's as though you slandered their mother. An example of this was clearly demonstrated when a woman was recently interviewed online about her personal experiences with her drug-addicted son. She was merely speaking about what she personally went through, but she dared to criticize pot and referred to it as a 'gateway' drug, which it was in her son's life. In response to her portrayal of marijuana as the factor that triggered the downward spiral of addiction in her son's life, marijuana lovers posted emotional comments that were absolutely off the charts. No facts were presented to prove her wrong, just intense emotional responses in defense of their precious 'best friend' – the drug that is always there to tell them the lie that they are doing just fine and have no worries.

Take note when you see people on television who speak in favor of legalizing marijuana. If you didn't know that they were talking about a drug, you could easily assume they were referring to their most dearly beloved family member. My twin daughters recently ran into an old high school acquaintance at the local convenience store. This guy is known to be a regular pot smoker. When they asked him how he was doing, he described to them the crisis point he and his long-time girl-friend had recently come to in their relationship. He had very honestly told his girlfriend that pot comes first in his life. He told her that he would never give it up even if it meant losing her. At least he was honest! His closest emotional relationship is with pot and he cannot foresee ever loving anyone more than he loves marijuana.

Something happens in the brain and emotional develop-ment of those who choose pot as their escape and/or coping mechanism. The effects of marijuana are insidious. On the surface the effects may not be as obvious as the effects of other drugs or alcohol. However, the person is changed in the way they see themselves in relation to other people. As a result, there are common relational characteristics that are demonstrated in the lives of regular pot smokers. One of these characteristics is a pattern of escapism when life gets challenging, uncomfortable or boring. This avoidance of difficulties leads to a lack or absence of maturity in response to life's issues and the people in their lives. There is a tendency to become either childlike or a bully in relationships, which are both signs of emotional immaturity. There seems to be no middle ground of dealing with and working through challenges. They will very conveniently blame the other person for any conflict that arises because if the other person just wouldn't worry about things, the conflict wouldn't exist. Pot has delivered them from having to work through emotional challenges. How convenient for them but how heartbreaking and frustrating for their loved ones (sometimes their children) who are carrying the burden of responsibility!

****

Most Christians are familiar with the verse that states "do not get drunk on wine, which leads to debauchery. Instead, be filled with the Spirit."[39] We are to make sure that the power of the Holy Spirit to speak to us and guide us is not being muffled or turned off. When the power and voice of the Holy Spirit is muffled within us, we are vulnerable to whatever traps and temptations come along. I used to drink casually and looked for loopholes in Scripture to justify my social drinking but several years ago I decided that I would rather err on the side of staying as clear-headed as possible at all times so that I could be sure to hear the voice and guidance of the Holy Spirit in any and every situation.

Every decision we make in life has great potential to bring blessing or harm on us and others. Allowing drugs or alcohol to influence our decision-making can lead to life-changing choices that we never would have made if we were completely clear-headed and sober. For example, I have met many young women who had their first sexual experience or had sex with someone they otherwise would not have, because they were under the influence of drugs or alcohol. Bristol Palin, in her book *Not Afraid of Life: My Journey So Far*[40] courageously admits that she doesn't even remember her first sexual experience. In a later interview, she clarified that the reason she doesn't remember is because she had gotten drunk that night for the first time. She had been committed to staying sexually pure till marriage until she turned over control of her thoughts and decisions to alcohol. This is just one example of the negative, life-changing effects of even *occasional* marijuana or *one-time* alcohol use. It becomes like – whatever!

****

As I spoke of before, one of the problems in our culture is that pot is not being treated as a dangerous drug that puts people at risk. For some mysterious reason, people who regularly smoke pot are not seen as addicts. In today's culture, addicts are either alcoholics or are addicted to harder drugs. I had someone recently say to me "Come on, we all did it when we were teenagers!" I looked at him and said "No. I didn't. And even if I did, does that disqualify me from discovering the truth about the effects of pot and attempting to protect my children from it?" It is not hypocritical to do everything in your power to keep your children from making the same mistakes you made as an adolescent or teen.

On television people wink and snicker about smoking pot like everyone does it and it's just funny. So many in this generation are learning to "cope" with challenges and bad feelings by smoking pot or drinking, or both, which is preventing them from successfully transitioning through this critical developmental stage into adulthood. As I stated before, the way we mature and grow emotionally is by going *through* difficulties.

James 1:2-4 bears repeating:

"Consider it pure joy, my brothers, whenever you face trials of many kinds because the testing of your faith develops perseverance. Perseverance must finish its work so that you may be mature and complete, not lacking anything."[41]

The struggle is what leads to emotional maturity. Avoiding the struggle leads to emotional immaturity or stagnation. Self-esteem and self-confidence come from working through the pain and hardship of the struggle and coming out the other side victorious, or at the very least, still standing. This critical developmental struggle is being subverted by marijuana and alcohol use. Good kids who won't touch alcohol or cigarettes are using pot, believing that it does no harm, just like Bobby in the example from Chapter 1.

I am seeing more and more young adults in their mid-20's who are still 14 or 15-years-old emotionally and are still smoking pot to cope with life. What a 'wonderful' drug! Promising young men and women are being sidelined to drift through life never even coming close to reaching their potential, dependent on others to be responsible for them emotionally even if they appear to be functioning in other ways, all due to marijuana use. The good feeling teenagers love about marijuana use also dulls their ability to discern danger or potential harm in a given situation. Pot robs them of their edge in decision-making and motivation, in exchange for a false sense of well-being. How sad for these young people, how sad for our country, and how very sad for the children they are bringing into the world.

****

A very interesting book was written by Chris Prentiss called *The Alcoholism and Addiction Cure.* In it, he presents a very different approach than what we are used to hearing and seeing regarding the treatment of addictions. He respectfully disagrees with the approach that says once an alcoholic or addict, always an alcoholic or addict. He believes that people can be cured of their addictions through a holistic approach that begins with the necessary step of uncovering, then treating the underlying cause. His own son, Pax, had a heroin addiction for 10 years and went through rehab after rehab, to no avail. In a poignant chapter of the book called "To Hell and Back," Pax describes the 10 years of hell he and his parents went through. Every time he relapsed, his father asked him why he was using drugs. He never had an answer beyond the fact that he was physically addicted. Finally, one day in yet another rehab facility, he was pondering that very question when he had an epiphany:

> "And then, in a flash, I had it! I knew why I was using heroin. It was as if the pearly gates had just opened and God had walked out and said, "Pax, my son, I'm going to free you from your addiction. I'm going to let you see why you've been using heroin and all the other drugs and alcohol for the past ten years." I absolutely knew why with every cell in my body!. . . I knew what lay behind my ten years of addiction."[42]

Pax described his epiphany to his father the next morning:

> "In essence, all I've been doing for the last ten years of my life is running away from fears. Drugs were my escape. They allowed me to feel the way I wanted to feel in life but wasn't able to. I knew that I always wanted to be a confident, strong, handsome, smart, capable person who could do anything, and that was what the drugs did for me. They allowed me to live out the fantasies about all the things I was afraid I wasn't capable of doing in real life."[43]

Our teenagers are turning to drugs and alcohol for a reason. It may be as simple as boredom and lack of purpose, but it is often much more complex. They need a purpose in life, something worth taking a risk for, something or someone greater than themselves who gives them significance, value and worth on this Earth.

WHAT CAN WE DO?

So what can we, as parents, do when the entire culture seems to be working against us in the realm of drinking, pot smoking, and even the use of harder drugs? I will offer specific strategies for parents to prepare young children and to help older kids battle back against the *Cultural Tsunami* in the second section of this book. Remember, it's not enough for teenagers to believe that drug and alcohol use are not a good thing. That belief will not carry them through life when they experience emotional pain and everyone else around them is using drugs, alcohol and/or sex to numb the pain and replace it with temporary pleasure. As we said before, pain pursues pleasure.

When we are preparing our children to face temptation, we need to approach drugs and alcohol in the same way we approached sexual immorality in the previous chapter. We need to ask ourselves what skills, characteristics and knowledge our children will need to possess within themselves to develop the desire, power and personal convictions to say no to alcohol and drug use when the temptation and opportunity are right in front of them. We *must* convey to our adolescents and teenagers from the very first conversation that we take any and all drug and alcohol use very seriously. A common mistake made by parents in America is that we often downplay what we believe to be experimentation with drugs and alcohol in the adolescent and teen years. Sometimes we even participate in this experimentation with our adolescents and teens believing that we are ushering them into adulthood. We often look at it as a necessary rite of passage that is part of the maturation process. The truth is, this experimentation actually stops the maturation process and ultimately costs many young people their very lives.

These very teens who are 'experimenting' are driving cars and engaging in other dangerous behaviors that not only put themselves at risk, but others as well. They are making decisions every day that have the potential to derail their very futures. And they are developing potentially lifelong habits that will affect generations to come. There is an ongoing argument in our culture about whether marijuana truly is a gateway drug. The truth is, I have never known or heard of anyone whose first experience with drugs was with cocaine or heroin. Of course, not every pot smoker will move on to harder drugs, but people who end up addicted to harder drugs started somewhere. Usually the first drug a person uses is alcohol or marijuana. People who begin drinking and doing drugs during the adolescent and teen years are at much higher risk of becoming alcoholics and addicts.[44] As noted earlier, young people who abstain from drugs and alcohol until they are 21 years old or older, are at very low risk of these behaviors becoming a debilitating factor in their lives.[45]

The best possible approach to preventing your son or daughter from becoming an addict is to talk about drugs and alcohol as they are growing up and to make it very clear as you are educating them that you absolutely will not tolerate them using these substances, even once. This is a hard sell if you have an alcohol cabinet in your home and a beer in your hand!

****

My son Chris, who was a regular pot smoker for many years, recently gave me the following list that represents his beliefs about marijuana and his reasons for quitting. Some of his points are arguable and slightly humorous; however, this list represents the beliefs of many in his generation. He explained to me that the many facts regarding the dangers of pot smoking that we, and most parents, have used to try to convince our children not to smoke are often not believed or taken seriously. I found his perspective to be very insightful:

- Pot cannot directly kill you no matter how much you smoke.
- Pot does not always lead to worse drugs.
- Pot does have proven medicinal uses.
- There is no real evidence that pot causes cancer, emphysema, or other ailments associated with cigarettes.
- Contrary to what you see in the movies, no girls will be attracted to you if you are a pothead.
- If you marry or enter into a relationship with a pothead girl, chances are she will eventually quit. If you continue to smoke, she will promptly ditch you for a non-pothead.
- Unless you plan on going into business for yourself or become a college professor, you will have to quit in order to be hired by almost any company.
- Even a small amount of pot can land you in jail on a first offense if you are busted by the wrong cop or put in front of the wrong judge who decides to make an example of you. This will follow you around for the rest of your life.
- If word gets out that you are a pothead, you will become a joke among your non-pothead peers and no one will take you seriously, even when you are not high.
- It's cool when Snoop does it. It's not cool when you do it. Don't ask me why because I don't know.
- It makes you feel more creative but it really makes you much, much less creative.

****

Parents I have worked with who discovered that their child was smoking pot or drinking fall into one of two categories. The first category is hesitant to take any action that will be too disruptive to their child's life, or to their own life. They don't want to 'over-react' and they certainly don't want to have to deal with an angry teenager. They are convinced that there has to be an easy way to deal with the situation. After all, it's just pot and/or beer. Talking to their child should be enough. The second category of parents takes their child's pot or alcohol use very seriously and is willing to do whatever it takes to stop their child from going down that road even one more day. These parents are willing to flip their child's world upside down and remove them from any opportunity to be with their peer group in social situations. It is a pleasure to work with this category of parents and there is almost always a positive end result. It can be a challenging road depending on how strongly the child reacts and how strong-willed the child is. It may even require that the parents remove their child from the school they are attending for a year or more. When the child realizes that his parents are just crazy enough to take drastic measures to keep him from using drugs or alcohol, he usually realizes it's just not worth it. Remember, at this point it's not essential that your child agrees with you that drugs and/or alcohol are harmful. The point is that they stop using.

Anyone who has a drug-addicted child can relate to the feeling that there is nothing you can do and that you might as well throw up your hands and give up. The reality is that we must not give up - especially if the drug-addicted child is an adolescent or teenager still living under our roof. We must stand strong and get all the help we can to respond to the challenge! Our children are worth it!

CHAPTER 5

THE SCHOOL EXPERIENCE

The typical adolescent and teenager in America spends 7 hours in school 5 days a week 9 months out of the year. Most teenagers have had this routine since they were 5 years old and some were in a daycare setting from infancy. Typically the prime hours of their day are spent in the school environment. American children and teenagers are being molded and socialized largely by their peers from a very young age. The American public school system is a cultural world all its own.

Teachers, more than any other group of adults besides parents, are on the front lines in the battle to save this generation. Some teachers take this challenge very seriously while others are out to take advantage of this powerful opportunity to indoctrinate our children and teens. Still others are apathetic. The worst scenario is when a bitter, resentful teacher remains in the classroom beyond his/her ability to be effective and daily takes out his/her frustration on the children under their care. Even if a school district recognizes that a teacher is ineffective or having a negative impact in the classroom, it is nearly impossible to fire them. The two main teachers' unions in America, the National Education Association (NEA) and the American Federation of Teachers (AFT), negotiate contracts on behalf of teachers which typically require the completion of about 23 steps in a nearly impossible time frame by school administrators before a tenured teacher can be fired. According to school reformer Geoffrey Canada, teachers are given tenure "basically just for breathing for 2-5 years."[46] Therefore, once a teacher has been given tenure (and given is the correct description since no requirements are demanded of a public school teacher to earn this tenure), they have job security.

The most recent deals made between the teachers unions in the state of New York, Mayor Bloomberg and Governor Cuomo in 2012 do not allow any public school teachers in the state to be fired for incompetence until June 2014. In addition, at the signing of this new deal, the slate is wiped clean for teachers who are currently in the process of being held accountable for poor student performance in their classrooms. Under the new deal, teachers must get "ineffective" ratings for two consecutive years before administrators can even begin the process toward dismissal.[47]

As noted in the highly-acclaimed documentary "Waiting for Superman," the state of Illinois has 876 school districts. At the time the documentary was produced, only 61 of these districts had ever attempted to fire a tenured teacher. Only 38 of those attempts were successful.[48] As a result of the contract rules that make it nearly impossible to fire a teacher, many administrators in school districts across America do what the Milwaukee School District calls "the dance of the lemons."[49] Principals will get together and rotate their "lemons" at the end of each school year in hopes that the lemons they get will be better than the lemons they are trading to another school. This is a little trick that also serves to calm down frustrated parents. Parents see ineffective teachers being 'removed' from their school and often don't realize that their ineffective teachers are being replaced by ineffective teachers from another school.

New York City has a unique way of dealing with problem teachers. For accusations ranging from excessive lateness to sexual offenses to plain old incompetence, teachers are sent to a Reassignment Center or "rubber room."[50] Up to 600 teachers spend 7 hours a day playing cards or reading the newspaper, all the while collecting their full salary and benefits. It can take up to three years for a disciplinary hearing to take place, which often results in the teacher being sent back to the classroom.

This system also hurts teachers who are unjustly accused of misconduct in the classroom. They sit in this rubber room waiting for a fair hearing for up to three years. The teachers in this Reassignment Center are costing the taxpayers of New York $100 million a year![51] Joel Klein, the Chancellor for New York City public schools in 2009 summed up his opinion of this system when he said: "You can never appreciate how irrational the system is until you've lived with it."[52] So whose interests are the NEA and AFT protecting? As Michelle Rhee, the Chancellor for the Washington, DC School District from 2007-2010 sums it up, "it has become all about the adults" when it comes to public schools in America.[53]

****

For reasons addressed in the chapters "Respect for Authority, or Lack Thereof" and "The Brick Wall of Authority," children in general are demonstrating less and less respect for authority. This, of course, has a profound effect on the environment in the average classroom. A teacher friend of mine who teaches at the elementary school level explained that many of her young students are expected to take on adult responsibilities at home. Often they are required to take care of younger siblings, make their own meals, make sure their siblings are fed, and basically figure out everything on their own with very little guidance. This makes it very difficult for these children to accept an adult authority figure telling them what to do and how to do it when they get to school.

A teacher friend of mine described how a fellow teacher trains the young children in her class to accept her authority – when she is first challenged, she stoops down to their level and calmly asks them to point to the person in charge. Most often they point to themselves. She then reminds them that she is in charge and has them point to her. She repeats this basic exercise many times before some of the students get it. Day after day she makes this point in a calm, non-confrontational manner then patiently waits for it to sink in.

Unfortunately, as teachers are respected less and less, the society continues to protect children from meaningful accountability and consequences. Spending a day or two in detention or in-school suspension is hardly a meaningful consequence. A high school teacher I know recently told me that part of the culture among teachers is to pacify or avoid parents. He reports that this carries over into the administration of many school districts as well. Teachers know that if they hold a student accountable, even for something as benign as turning in an assignment on time, they run the risk of having a parent in their face for not giving their kid a break.

****

It is completely unacceptable but understandable that bullying has become an epidemic in schools and on school buses today. With the breakdown of respect for authority and parents going after teachers who attempt to hold their children accountable, who is drawing the line as far as students' behavior in public schools? Without clear, immoveable limits, societies become uncivilized. I recently read an article about two different bullying situations. In the first situation, a father allegedly paid a student to beat up the girl who was bullying his daughter. In the second situation, a mother actually physically attacked the boy who was bullying her child. Both of these parents said that the schools had been told repeatedly about the bullying and had done nothing to stop it. The problem is the schools don't have the authority to do much of anything besides assigning the student to a few days of detention. Public schools are hesitant to expel students because the school district is still responsible financially for providing an education for the expelled student. As a result, when they expel a student they end up paying in some other way for the child's education.

I personally know a few school bus drivers. They have told me many outrageous stories of bullying and sexual harassment by students on their buses and the disrespect they deal with as school bus drivers. School bus drivers are only allowed to do so much when it comes to controlling the children on their buses. It's no wonder bus companies have placed video cameras on school buses. This generation of parents seems so invested in protecting their children from responsibility and consequences that they typically do not take action when told that their child is a bully. Many parents refuse to accept that their child is the problem and blame the school, the teacher, the bus driver or other students. The end result is chaos with no one drawing a line in the sand that stops this type of behavior.

It's as though the culture considers absolute, unwavering requirements placed on a child to be cruel and unusual punishment. Rules are expected to be bent or broken to prevent children and teens from experiencing any level of discomfort or negative consequence for their choices. As a result, many teachers have become cynical and treat all parents as if they are the enemy. This works against well-meaning parents who are genuinely trying to advocate for their child's best interest. Instead of teachers and parents working together in the best interest of the students, the teacher/parent relationship is fraught with cynicism and defensiveness on both sides.

On the other side of this coin, I know an amazing family that adopted three siblings out of an extremely neglectful situation. They already had two older biological children in the home. These parents worked very hard to figure out which disciplinary approach worked most effectively with each of their adopted children. The children did not respond to time outs or other measures typically used with children these days. They discovered that one of the children only responded to clear, firm rules and consistent, meaningful consequences for disobedience. A gentle, compassionate approach is not effective with this particular child. The parents had a daily, uphill battle with the school as teachers undermined this approach at every turn. No matter how hard the parents attempted to explain their approach to the school, they were viewed as being too hard on the child. I should clarify that no physical punishment was being advocated or used by these parents. When the school called the parents to report noncompliance on the part of their child, the parents would ask what consequence the child was given by the school. The school was resistant to responding in a stern, decisive, consistent manner. They expressed disagreement with the parents' methods, expressed pity for the child and in the process crippled him further. The school obviously believed they knew better than the parents what was best for this child.

This attitude was clearly demonstrated at a hearing that was held in February of 2012 by the Michigan House Education Committee. At this hearing, Debbie Squires, Director of the Michigan Elementary and Middle Schools Principals Association, stated: "Educators are the people who know best about how to serve children, that's not necessarily true of an individual resident." She went on to say, "I'm not saying they don't want the best for their children, but they may not know what actually is best. . . "[54] The purpose of this hearing was to discuss school choice issues, in particular parents who want the freedom to send their children to charter schools. Unfortunately, teachers and administrators have often become so deeply entrenched in a turf and respect battle with parents that meaningful education has, at times, gone by the wayside.

****

The average teacher spends hours and hours each week preparing lesson plans and grading papers, usually on their own time. When they are in the classroom, a great deal of their time is often spent in classroom management. In many classrooms, very little time is effectively spent actually teaching the subject at hand. Many times, students come to class unprepared. The typical student does not have very high expectations of their academic experience and believes that school is a complete waste of their time. Therefore, for a middle school or high school teacher to be effective in an average classroom, he or she must be a confident disciplinarian and a creative person who can think on their feet, possess boundless energy each and every day, and be capable of keeping their own focus as well as the attention of 30 adolescents or teenagers. All of this amid a multitude of distractions for 50 or more minutes only to turn around and do the same thing 10 minutes later with a new set of 30 or more students.

Not surprisingly, many teachers have all but given up the fight. They often become content with mediocrity and many are at a loss as to how to handle their classrooms. This isn't what they signed up for when they were idealistic twenty-somethings fresh out of college. We often send them into the battle without the tools they need to be successful. We expect them to teach students who have very little, if any, respect for the teacher's position of authority in the classroom and care very little about learning. When a teacher attempts to require respect from their students and one parent complains, the typical response from the administration is not one of support for the teacher. Typically the teacher is required to back down. Some students enter the classroom with one agenda – to rattle the teacher and entertain their fellow students.

Imagine going to your job every day and being faced with constant attempts to undermine your effectiveness, day in and day out, with no available recourse. Teachers are the ones on the front lines in the education of our children but only the strongest, most creative, energetic and motivated teachers are capable of rising to the top in today's educational environment. Charter, private and independent schools are often more successful because in most cases they have the freedom to make their own rules without union interference and are able to expel children who refuse to comply with behavioral rules. Involved parents have known for a couple of generations that the public school system in America is broken. I believe, as it is structured today, the American public school system is dying a slow, torturous death.

I remember being bored silly in high school. I coasted through with B's and C's and hardly ever studied. In my third year of college I was suddenly turned on to learning and academic achievement. It was the first time that I was really challenged in a way that caught my interest. What a great feeling and sense of accomplishment when I got straight A's for the first time. So many high school students are bored to death and see absolutely no relevance to their lives in the classroom. What a shame! We are finding out as a culture what happens when you throw together several hundred teenagers every day who see absolutely no purpose or significance behind the behavioral and academic expectations being placed on them. Quite often, it's not a pretty picture.

****

A true story that illustrates just how bad the situation has gotten in many public schools is the story of a 13-year-old girl I'll call "Jessica." Jessica was a sensitive girl who attended a large public middle school in a suburban area. She had a particularly difficult 7th grade year during which she had developed anxiety issues that almost paralyzed her socially and seemed to revolve around social pressures in school. Jessica had no one in her social circle who shared her lunch time so she often found herself sitting alone at lunch, which can be devastating for kids at that age. She also had a science teacher who terrified her. He overcompensated for students' lack of respect for authority by yelling and berating them for the entire hour they were in his classroom. Jessica was positioned in the front row and he often pounded on her desk as he yelled at the class. Jessica's parents spoke with the guidance office and, to the school's credit, they asked the teacher to move Jessica to a different area of the classroom. One of the guidance counselors made herself available to talk to Jessica anytime she felt overwhelmed. This helped her get through 7ᵗʰ grade.

When 8ᵗʰ grade came around, Jessica had determined that she was going to force herself to be more outgoing socially and make as many friends as possible. She was not going to have a repeat of 7ᵗʰ grade. One of her school friends was a young man who was funny and very popular with everyone. I'll call him Scott. Scott's father was a teacher at the school so students and teachers alike seemed to know and like Scott. He was a class clown and always had the kids laughing. No one seemed to take him too seriously. He was a star athlete and liked Jessica very much. They had all of their classes together and spent most of every school day together. Scott was just the security blanket that Jessica needed. Having Scott around helped Jessica to have a much more positive social experience at school since Scott's friends also became Jessica's friends. They saw each other occasionally outside of school when they were with their group of friends, but never alone. Scott asked Jessica to be more than friends on more than one occasion, but she always said no and made it clear to him that she just wanted to be friends with him.

Jessica heard comments from some of the girls regarding sexual experiences they claimed to have had with Scott so she knew that he had a reputation for acting out sexually. The other kids laughed about the stories that were told and the sexual comments Scott made about girls at school. Jessica was uncomfortable with this side of Scott, but her relationship with Scott was different and was limited to the school building. When Valentine's Day rolled around, Scott gave her flowers that a club at the school had for sale in the school lobby along with a ring. He asked her, once again, to be his girlfriend. She thanked him for the gifts but clearly said no, once again.

Jessica's parents knew Scott was a popular kid at the school and that his father was a well-respected teacher. They didn't see any reason to be concerned for Jessica's safety in the school building. None of the parents they knew had indicated any concerns about Scott's behavior. Jessica told her parents about the flowers and the ring. They thought it was sweet and thought that Jessica handled the situation well. She had also gotten flowers from a boy in the neighborhood and had handled that situation in much the same way. The main thing they were noticing was how happy Jessica was this year as opposed to her 7th grade year. This group of friends she had at school seemed to be a positive influence in her life, and her social life was limited to school and sports activities, so there wasn't much opportunity for anything bad to happen. After all, she was safe during the school day inside the school building – or so they thought.

It was a normal day in the spring of Jessica's 8th grade year, except that her mother was home early from work. Jessica came in the door at the usual time, having ridden the school bus home. She was surprised that her mother was home and immediately broke down crying. Through her tears, she began spilling out the details of what happened at school that day. It all started in 3rd period, when Jessica realized she had left something in her locker. She asked the teacher if she could retrieve it. The teacher consented and as Jessica left the classroom, Scott asked if he could accompany her. Once again, the teacher gave his approval. Jessica was happy for the company as she had to walk quite a distance through hallways and stairwells to get to her locker. On the way through mostly deserted hallways, Scott began asking her if he could kiss her. Jessica adamantly said no. The questions and pestering continued. Jessica began to walk faster and repeatedly said no. She began telling Scott to leave her alone. Then they entered a deserted stairwell. Scott grabbed Jessica and pinned her against the wall. In a few seconds that later seemed like a blur, Scott began forcibly kissing and putting his hands all over Jessica. At one point he had his hand up her skirt and at another point he had a hand on her breast. Jessica made as much noise as she could and fought back. After a few seconds of molestation, Scott let her go then continued to follow her to her locker.

Jessica's mind was reeling. She practically ran the rest of the way to her locker, got what she needed, then continued quickly back toward her classroom. Scott continued to follow, begging her to not be angry with him. At one point, Jessica forcefully ordered Scott to walk on the other side of the hallway. Scott complied. Jessica went back into class and sat quietly until class was over.

Now, from our vantage point we might question why Jessica didn't go directly to the Principal's office and report what had just happened. The reality was that her mind hadn't processed what had just occurred and she was completely in shock, unable to decide what to do in that moment. As a result, she went into the mode of continuing with the routine of the day, almost like she was on auto pilot. Lunch period was next on the schedule. Jessica didn't wait for Scott, as she usually did, and quickly got with her group of female friends. She immediately told them what had just happened and they surrounded her as Scott attempted to get to her.

Suddenly it began sinking in to Scott that Jessica may report what had just happened. During lunch period, Jessica formulated a plan to talk to Mrs. Smith, the one teacher she completely trusted, as soon as she got to that classroom. As she was getting books out of her locker after lunch period, Scott came up behind her and punched his fist into the locker next to her head. His attitude had gone from pleading to threatening. Finally, Jessica woke up and realized she had to do something now. She ran into Mrs. Smith's classroom and told her that she needed to talk. Mrs. Smith went into the hallway with her and heard the entire story. Jessica and Mrs. Smith were both in tears as Mrs. Smith accompanied her to the Vice Principal's office.

Of course, in the time that had passed between the incident and telling Mrs. Smith, word had spread like wildfire that something had happened between Jessica and Scott. Scott's father caught wind of it and immediately went looking for Jessica. He found Jessica and Mrs. Smith heading to the office. He stopped them and demanded that Jessica come into a room alone with him. If it were not for Mrs. Smith protecting her, Jessica would have most likely been verbally assaulted by Scott's father in an attempt to intimidate her into not telling on Scott. Mrs. Smith was a Godsend for Jessica as she stood up to Scott's father and refused to let him speak to Jessica.

Now, wouldn't we all assume that the minute this incident was brought to the attention of the Vice Prin-cipal, Jessica's parents would be called? Isn't that why we fill out those emergency contact forms at the beginning of every school year listing about three different people who can be contacted in case of an emergency during the school day? Well, this is where the story gets interesting. The school's response is very telling and unfortunately, based on reports from parents and my own observations, somewhat common. No parent was called. The administration immediately went into damage control mode, putting the best interest of the school district first. Jessica's story was taken and she was sent back to class to finish out the school day and ride home on the bus. This gave the Vice Principal time to figure out what to do before any parents were involved. Outrageous! Scott was called to the office. Of course his father was there running interference for him. Scott shed a few tears, said that Jessica had led him on and that he thought she was teasing him when she was running away saying no. He expressed bitter remorse, was given 10 days of in-school suspension and was told to write a letter of apology to Jessica. As far as the school was concerned, this was the end of the story. They hadn't heard from Jessica's parents yet!

When Jessica arrived home and told her mother what had happened, her mother immediately called the school, demanding to speak with the Vice Principal. They were told that she was meeting with the Superintendent and couldn't be reached. Well, of course she had gone to the Superintendent's office to report the incident and get her orders for how to handle the situation in the best interest of the school district. She knew there wasn't much time until the parents would know what had happened. The parents demanded to have her contacted on her cell phone and finally spoke with her about an hour after their first contact with the school. A meeting was set up for first thing the next morning. The parents were assured that Scott would be in In School Suspension (ISS) the next day and would not be allowed to have any contact with Jessica. Jessica wanted to go to school the next day so her parents let her since they had been assured that Scott would not have access to Jessica. As Jessica walked into the cafeteria the next morning to get a bagel and meet her friends, there was Scott getting breakfast before reporting to ISS! One more indication of how seriously the school was taking the matter. Once again her friends encircled her as Scott tried to get to her to beg her not to get him into any more trouble.

The school's position on the incident was that it was just a misunderstanding between teenagers that often happens "at this age." Scott meant no harm and, after all, Jessica had on a rather short skirt that day. Scott was remorseful and cried when he was in the Vice Principal's office. He had obviously learned an important lesson. The school was sure it would never happen again. And, after all, Scott's father was a teacher himself so he could be trusted to make sure Scott behaved himself in the future. Jessica's parents were not pacified by this interpretation of events. They called their lawyer and the police and pressed charges against Scott.

Jessica bravely told and retold her story in precise detail as she was questioned several times by law enforcement. The school was told by Jessica's parents to back off and cooperate or they would be sued. In the process of taking the incident through the legal system, it became known that Scott had other past sexual offenses on his record that were sealed due to his age. He was charged with, and plead guilty to 5 counts of indecent sexual assault. Jessica stood up in a courtroom and read a statement she had prepared telling Scott, his parents, and the court how this incident had affected her. Scott was required to move in with his mother in another school district, was put on probation for a year and required to attend an intensive, year-long treatment program for juvenile sexual offenders. In his psycho-sexual evaluation, it was stated that he was at high risk for being a repeat offender. In fact, he was already a repeat offender. We can only imagine what he would have done to his next victim, if no one intervened.

That wasn't the end of the story for Jessica and her family. Jessica, who insisted on returning to school instead of going on homebound instruction for the remaining three months of the school year, endured icy stares, an empty seat in every classroom where Scott used to sit, comments around her about how the Lacrosse team was suffering because Scott was no longer there, and even comments from girls who admitted to having similar experiences with Scott but told Jessica that it was no big deal, insinuating that Jessica had overreacted. Jessica's mother was even confronted by a Lacrosse parent who told her that because of Jessica their Lacrosse team was losing all their games. Rumors were flying around the school and the community, spreading mostly false information. The rumors typically presented Scott as the victim of an overly emotional girl!

****

What can we learn about the public school culture from this single incident? I believe there is a wealth of valuable information in this example that can assist us in understanding many underlying truths that are foundational to the functioning of public schools every day in America. A few of the most obvious observations are:

- There are many wonderful teachers in today's public schools. Mrs. Smith is a perfect example of this fact. She cared about Jessica and that was all that mattered to her in that moment.
- There are many wonderful students in today's public schools. Many of Jessica's friends rallied around her when she needed them most.

- Women and girls are still being blamed when they are assaulted. "Boys will be boys" is still alive and well, which is an insult to both sexes.
- Teenage girls often do not believe they deserve to be respected and are quite often willing to sacrifice themselves to please boys, as was demonstrated by the girls who tolerated Scott's sexual advances.
- Teenage boys are often just as confused and misled as teenage girls.
- When it comes down to it, public schools seem to be first and foremost concerned with self-preservation.
- Teenagers often seem more concerned with being "chill" as though they don't really care about anything, than with standing up for what is right. Taking a personal risk is rarely valued in the youth culture, unless it's a physical risk involving sports. Standing up for unpopular beliefs is often not valued, and is frequently punished by peers. In the lives of today's teens, emotional risk just doesn't seem worth it.
- Parents are often, themselves, emotionally immature and are often caught up in getting their own needs met through their children. As a result, many parents aren't up to the task of building character in the next generation.
- Many parents are invested in making excuses for their children's behavior and protecting their children from experiencing consequences for their actions.
- Public school administrators are often invested in talking the talk but not walking the walk when it comes to partnering with parents in the best interest of their children.
- School administrators and teachers are frequently engaged in a turf battle with parents. There is very little, if any, mutual trust or respect between schools and parents. Kids are getting lost in the middle.

****

Entire books have been written exploring the causes behind the breakdown of public education in America. As previously cited, the excellent documentary, "Waiting for Superman,"[55] is a must-see for anyone interested in this subject. There seems to be a consensus that our country is falling behind when it comes to effectively educating our children. There have been a multitude of solutions suggested from all sides of this issue. I will discuss two of those options in Chapter 16. I firmly believe that the traditional public school system, as we know it, cannot survive unless significant change occurs. I would even venture to say that perhaps the traditional public school system as it is currently structured isn't worth saving.

I believe it's time for a radical restructuring to occur in the educational system in America. As I'm writing this, the new Governor here in the state of Pennsylvania is proposing vast spending cuts to the state's educational system. Many teachers and parents are very upset by these proposed cuts. The idea is that if you care about education and children you will automatically increase each year the amount of money the state and federal governments are doling out. If you don't, then you obviously don't care about the children. After all, doesn't more money equal a better education? Not necessarily! The facts are that real spending per student increased by 23.5 percent in the decade between 1998 and 2008 and by 49 percent in the 20 years between 1988 and 2008.[56] However, "long-term measures of American students' academic achievement, such as long-term NAEP reading scale scores and high school graduation rates, show that the performance of American students has not improved dramatically in recent decades, despite substantial spending increases."[57]

My belief is that there needs to be a restructuring so that schools are "lean and mean" in their approach to spending the money they currently have. Teachers and administrators absolutely should be well-paid; however, they must be held accountable to a very high standard and districts should be able to fire ineffective teachers. We are entrusting them with tremendous influence over the lives and futures of our children! We also must reinstate a structure that grants teachers the authority they need to do their job. Children must be expected to treat their teachers with respect whether they want to or not, and whether their parents have taught them to respect authority or not. School administrators must back up their teachers when students are disrespectful and disruptive. When teachers no longer have to fight for basic respect from their students, they will be free to actually teach.

It's time to explore new and more effective ways of educating our children that take into account the changing needs of teenagers in a rapidly-evolving culture. Just maybe, throwing hundreds or even thousands of teenagers together for 7 or 8 hours a day in an environment where respect has broken down and the authority figures are often powerless and sometimes cynical, is no longer an effective way of providing the best possible education for our children.

When a teenage girl can be sexually molested in the stairwell of a public middle school in the middle of the day and the school administrators, many students and parents think it's no big deal, the public school culture is no longer civilized. It seems to me that Columbine symbolically signaled the death knell for traditional public schools. It's time for an honest, unflinching look at the state of public education in America.

WHAT CAN WE DO?

It really does come down to us as parents. We must take back responsibility for the education and upbringing of our children. We are the ones who have to answer to God for the children He has placed in our lives. It's time for us to get out of our comfort zone and do the sacrificial work of first training our children in the biblical truths that are the foundation of life. We must require obedience and respect from our children, first toward us as their parents, then toward other authority figures, and ultimately toward God. We must hold our children accountable for their actions and resist coddling them or making excuses for their disrespectful behaviors. We must also take back the responsibility for our children's academic education. They are capable of learning so much more than we typically expect of them.

Educational options are available in the United States, from homeschooling with the support of homeschool groups to charter schools to private schools to online schools. If you decide on public or private school for your child, you must be actively involved and know what's going on in your child's school. It's a personal decision that every parent has to make for their own child. If our children are going to stand strong in this world, we must give them the best possible education, both academically and morally, in an environment that does not threaten the very foundation we are attempting to build deep within them. It's not up to the school. It's not up to the church. It's not up to the government. It's up to us, the parents!

CHAPTER 6

DIVORCE

The vast majority of today's teens have unmet emotional and psychological needs, especially if their parents are divorced or separated. These teenagers have experienced instability, rejection, and abandonment, whether their parents attempted to shield them from these emotional wounds or not. The fact of the matter is that when a child's parents divorce, there is typically instability prior to the divorce as the parents fight or drift apart. Then there are instability and feelings of rejection and abandonment when the divorce occurs. Following the divorce, grief sets in as the child misses whichever parent they are not with at the moment. In many cases, one or both parents begin dating and often one or both remarry which brings a step-parent and often step-siblings into the picture.

One couple I worked with was confused by the behavior of the woman's five-year-old child from her previous marriage. The little girl had experienced the divorce of her parents when she was three, then both parents remarried bringing step-siblings into her life. I drew a diagram for the mother and step-father detailing this little girl's complicated life with all of the different, new relationships she had to navigate in two very different homes that she moved between every few days. It was no wonder this precious little girl was exhibiting unusual behavior. She was attempting to find a solid place to stand in all of the confusion that was her life. Nothing around her stayed stable for any length of time.

Stability is everything to a child. From birth to adulthood, children go through developmental stages that involve every part of their being – emotional, psychological, spiritual and physical. The success of this process depends greatly on the stability of the family foundation that supports them. The family unit is intended to provide the consistency, security, unconditional love, and acceptance that are the building blocks of this foundation. When parents divorce the rug is pulled out from under the children. There is nothing a parent can do to prevent the child of divorce from experiencing the very foundation of their life being shaken beneath them. For the rest of their lives children of divorce are searching for solid ground to stand on. Their ability to trust is shaken to the point that they often experience serious relational problems into adulthood.

****

Our culture is still reverberating from the effects of the feminist movement of the 1960's. Betty Friedan, the author of *The Feminine Mystique*, is credited with igniting the women's movement with her book's publication in 1963. She had picked up on a very real phenomenon in our culture at that time. Many women truly felt unfulfilled and dissatisfied with their lives. They were bored and unhappy and were longing for purpose. Friedan described it as "the problem that has no name."[58] She defined this problem as a voice within women that was saying "I want more than my husband and my children and my home."[59] The leaders of the feminist movement believed they had found the answer in the differences between men and women. Since the feminist leadership was not looking to God for solutions, I believe they arrived at a logical, worldly conclusion. They then set out with self-righteous fervor to convince society that men had all the advantages and that, if women were going to be fulfilled, they had to chase after and lay claim to the advantages and perceived freedom that men supposedly were enjoying. The sad truth is that men were and are struggling to find the same fulfillment and purpose as women. They just approach the struggle differently due to basic biological differences between the genders.

Doors that were previously closed to women were opened in large part by the feminist movement and society has benefited from the contributions of women in the workplace and other leadership positions. However, the path laid out by the feminist movement has decimated homes, families and individuals in the process. And, interestingly enough, the exact same "problem that has no name"[60] is still stirring in the hearts and souls of women. Come to think of it, I think this "problem that has no name"[61] was quite possibly beating in the heart and soul of Eve at the beginning of all creation. Eve fell for Satan's lie that she was being deprived of something and if only she ate the fruit that was forbidden by God she would experience complete knowledge and fulfillment. Today, the culture would define the problem as a voice within women saying "I want more than my boyfriend, husband, children, home, career, etc. etc."

Where I believe Friedan and the feminist movement went wrong was to blame the priority women gave to the role of caregiver of their homes and families as the root cause of this unhappiness and deep lack of fulfillment. Of course, to the feminists the obvious answer was for women to refuse to make home and family their top priority. Someone else can be paid to take care of the home and the children. The husband can take care of himself. Women were encouraged to make their own personal happiness and fulfillment their top priority. The idea was that women were unfulfilled because they were putting the needs of others ahead of their own needs and wants. Once again, this sounds very much like the self-centered struggle that occurred in the Garden of Eden as described in the book of Genesis in the Bible.

Feminists encouraged women to seek the respect of the world by having a job in the community and climbing the corporate ladder. I give the feminist leadership the benefit of the doubt that they truly believed that they had the answers women were seeking. Women were also encouraged to shake off the guilt and shame of casual sex (and its consequences) because it was believed that they were missing out on the sexual freedom that men were supposedly enjoying. Also, women were told it wasn't fair that they got saddled with the chief responsibility for raising the children and taking care of the home. There's no glory in that! To make casual sex and freedom from responsibility for children acceptable, the culture had to make birth control available and abortion legal and accessible. Then the culture had to fight long and hard to convince women that they had no reason to feel shame or guilt for choosing their own selfish ambition and desires over the very lives and needs of their children. The old adage "the hand that rocks the cradle, rules the world" was thrown out the window as baloney. Unfortunately, women and society did not realize or acknowledge the profound position of influence women had in the home that impacted generations to come. Many women bought the lie, originated in the pit of hell, that chasing after their own happiness, fulfillment and respect in the eyes of the world would give them that certain something they were missing. Look where that lie has taken us!

Today's mothers are often extremely overwhelmed by a multitude of responsibilities. Many children are placed in daycare from a very young age. When they are picked up at the end of their parents' work day, they are rushed home, fed, bathed and put to bed only to begin the process again very early the next morning. Weekends are spent playing catch-up with grocery shopping, house cleaning, and parents trying to have a social life. When kids are old enough to be home alone, parents often rejoice at the tremendous financial relief of no daycare bill each month. Many parents also celebrate a new sense of personal freedom when their children are older and seem to need less supervision. The reality is that adolescents and teens need just as much, if not more, of their parents' availability and supervision. More than half of today's parents have given up on at least one marriage.

They are sometimes investing time and energy chasing their own sexual and relational fulfillment at the expense of their children. Teenagers have frequently gotten lost in the shuffle of blended families. Which child belongs to which parent often becomes a diluted concept.

So where does that leave our marriages, our children and our homes? It doesn't take a rocket scientist to see how the solutions provided by the feminist movement have contributed to the unstable home environments the last two generations of children have grown up in. Home and family are no longer at the top of the list of priorities. Women and men alike are often quick to leave marriage and family if they feel unfulfilled or unhappy. The brutally honest conclusions drawn by Bennett and Ellison in their previously cited *Newsweek* article speak to the opinions held by many young adults today regarding marriage. They state that:

". . . 40 years after the feminist movement established our rights in the workplace, a generation after the divorce rate peaked, and a decade after *Sex and the City* made singledom chic, marriage is – from a legal and practical standpoint, at least - no longer necessary."[62]

The authors' description of the typical style of upbringing experienced by their contemporaries is very telling:

"Boomers may have been the first children of divorce, but ours is a generation for whom multiple households were the norm. We grew up shepherded between bedrooms, minivans, and dinner tables, with step-parents, half-siblings, and highly complicated holiday schedules. You can imagine then – amid incessant high-profile adultery scandals – that we'd be somewhat cynical about the institution. (Till death do us part, really?)"[63]

Is it any wonder that so many of today's teenagers and young adults are searching for personal significance and value? Often they are not made to feel valuable and significant in the early years as they are shuttled between homes and to and from daycare providers. Many parents don't know how to find fulfillment and purpose in their own lives having bought into the misguided promises offered by the culture. All their kids know is what they've seen their parents do. What have we done, as parents, that has clearly shown our teenagers the path to a fulfilling life that deserves to be emulated and respected? Have we shown our teenagers, in our own marriage relationship, what true love and intimacy look like? If not, why would they believe that a marriage relationship is worth waiting and sacrificing for?

Have you ever heard a teenager say "I want to have a marriage just like my parents'?" It's the rare teenager who feels that way. Typically, teenagers are looking to avoid the pitfalls their parents fell into. Many have no desire to marry because they see no hope that the promise of commitment will be fulfilling and will last. The bottom line is they don't trust anyone to love them completely and unconditionally and to honor the commitment of marriage and family. If their own parents couldn't, why would they believe anyone could or would? So then, what do teenagers do? They get whatever human connection they can, which usually means sex. Casual sex gives an emotionally needy, insecure person a sense of emotional and physical connection, if only for a few moments. For girls it mimics love and a feeling of being special. For boys it brings sex down to a basic physical connection and takes away any sense of a special bond shared only with one person.

I don't necessarily blame the feminist leadership for the breakdown of families. They took a very real issue – a lack of fulfillment and purpose that many women were feeling in the 1950's and 1960's - and attempted to identify the problem and provide a solution on behalf of the sisterhood. The problem only grew when they looked for the solution horizontally rather of vertically. We will always ultimately end up creating more dissatisfaction for ourselves when we look around us for solutions that do not exist in the physical realm. Yes, we may find temporary excitement and happiness from the world's solutions, but when we sit alone in the quiet darkness of night the emptiness is still within us. The answer to this "problem that has no name"[64] is Jesus Christ. Only a personal relationship with Jesus Christ can bring peace, contentment and fulfillment to the depth of our being. The fulfillment that Jesus gives transcends our circumstances and human relationships.

****

A landmark 25-year longitudinal study on the effects of divorce was conducted and the results compiled in the book *The Unexpected Legacy of Divorce* by Judith S. Wallerstein, Julia M. Lewis, and Sandra Blakeslee. I believe that the divorce rate would drop substantially if every parent considering divorce would read this book. Wallerstein described this work as "the only study in the world that follows into full adulthood the life course of individuals whose parents separated when they were young children."[65] Wallerstein recruited a core group of 131 children and their families in 1971. She carefully screened the participants and chose children who were doing relatively well in school and did not have pre-existing developmental problems.

Wallerstein followed these children closely, conducting in-depth interviews with them and both of their parents at least every five years. In their final interviews, she was able to locate 80% of the now grown children and conducted face-to-face interviews. These adult children were between the ages of 28-43 at the time of their final interviews. For contrast, Wallerstein also conducted "extended interviews with a comparison group of adults from intact families who were the same age and were raised in the same neighborhoods and schools as those in the long-term study of divorced families."[66] Wallerstein includes chapters in her book entitled "When a Child Becomes the Caregiver," "Growing Up Is Harder," "Growing Up Lonely," "Court-Ordered Visiting, The Child's View," "The Vulnerable Child," and "Is Not Fighting Enough." Children of divorce are bound to see themselves in the pages of this comprehensive work. Her findings were profound and her results are beyond argument because they came straight from those who lived it.

After studying children of divorce for over 30 years, Wallerstein believes that "we've created a new kind of society never before seen in human culture. Silently and unconsciously, we have created a culture of divorce."[67] Our society is ambivalent about divorce. Many seem to celebrate the freedom that no-fault divorce offers as fewer people feel trapped in the commitment of marriage. If we believe we have made a mistake when we chose the person we married, we can easily back ourselves out of this commitment and move on to the next relationship. As I have been told by more than one client in my office, "You can't expect me to stay in a relationship that makes me unhappy!" Wallerstein clearly describes the situation we have created:

> "The sobering truth is that we have created a new kind of society that offers greater freedom and more opportunities for many adults, but this welcome change carries a serious hidden cost. Many people, adults and children alike, are in fact not better off. We have created new kinds of families in which relationships are fragile and often unreliable. Children today receive far less nurturance, protection, and parenting than was their lot a few decades ago. Long-term marriages come apart at still surprising rates. And many in the older generation who started the divorce revolution find themselves estranged from their adult children."[68]

You may be contemplating divorce and thinking to yourself that you will handle things differently than most parents. You will be the couple that ends their marriage in a civil fashion with no fighting over custody and no fighting in front of the children. Perhaps you have already been very careful to avoid conflict in front of your children, believing that you are sparing them the heartache that other children experience. You're determined that your children will not suffer and will actually be better off after the divorce because you will be happier. Judith Wallerstein addresses this type of 'perfect' divorce situation from the perspective of one of the children in her study that lived it – Lisa. During and after Lisa's parents' divorce, Lisa was extremely well-behaved in school and seemed to have adjusted beautifully to the changes in her family situation. However, she became increasingly fearful at night and needed the lights left on. As Wallerstein spent one-on-one time with Lisa, this precious little girl expressed grief, pain and concern over the loss of her family. As Wallerstein describes it:

> "Neither parent was aware of the extent of Lisa's grief and pain over the divorce. She seemed so self-controlled, so calm. Surely, they told themselves, her fears will disappear in time. Actually, they lasted for several years and worsened again when her mother took on a heavier work schedule. That's when Lisa began to worry daily that her mother would die."[69]

Parent and child relationships always change after a divorce. Parents, out of necessity, are required to focus on entirely new life situations and problems. Often one or both parents must move and complex financial and custody situations must be resolved. Sometimes mothers are forced to go to work for the first time or increase their hours on the job. This often results in much less time and focus being placed on the child and his or her emotional and psychological needs, which during and after a divorce are growing and changing. Even if there is limited outward conflict between the parents, the child's world is turned upside down and they most often receive less time and attention from both parents. Children see their parents struggling and stressed and often keep their fears and concerns to themselves, not wanting to add to the tension in the family. This response is often misconstrued as resilience, and the parents pat themselves on the back for handling their divorce in a way that did not upset their child. In reality, the child is suffering in silence.

****

In recent months I have gotten to know the most amazing young couple – I will call them Joanie and Jim. Joanie and Jim first came to my office to discuss their concerns over the behavior of their 4-year-old son, Mark. Jim was working a demanding full-time job, Joanie was working full-time as a nurse and taking classes toward an advanced degree, and they had a 7-month-old baby boy named Jordan. Mark and Jordan were attending a wonderful, full-time daycare center/preschool run by a local church. Mark had recently begun acting out in an aggressive manner toward other children. This was very much out of character for Mark, so these parents sought my counsel.

Now the most obvious explanation for Mark's recent change in behavior would be the birth of a new baby brother, which had turned his world upside down. I have no doubt that a new baby in the family after being the only child for almost 4 years was life changing for Mark. However, as I dug deeper over the next few weeks, this young couple confessed that they were barely holding their marriage together. They each expressed anger and resentment toward the other over relatively small offenses and they were both deeply hurt by the anger and resentment being directed at them. As I explored this young couple's life together, no major offenses could be found. Each worked diligently and each loved their children and only wanted the best for them.

Given that the most immediate concern was Mark's behavior at preschool, I inquired of Joanie if it was feasible for her to postpone her schooling so that she would have more time to focus on Mark's needs. It was not feasible for Jim to cut back his hours or leave his job as he was the main bread-winner. Joanie expressed disappointment at the thought, as she was driven to complete her degree; however, she was willing to put her child's needs first. She immediately dropped out of school. Jim was challenged to spend more time with Mark, including him in projects around the house and giving him one-on-one attention. Jim agreed.

Over the next couple weeks, Jim reluctantly expressed that he had always pictured a situation for his children where their mother was home with them during the day. I explored this possibility with both parents and Joanie admitted that she had always wanted to be home with her young children as well. However, she was afraid of losing the job she loved. As Jim and Joanie discussed this possibility, and the fact that it would only be temporary until the children were in school full-time, Joanie approached her employer. As it turned out, the employer was willing to keep Joanie on the schedule one day a week until she was ready to increase her hours. Joanie left her full-time position and withdrew both children from daycare/preschool.

All of these changes happened in a very short period of time. The first month was a period of adjustment. Joanie had always been an over-achiever who pushed herself to meet rather lofty goals. She had watched her mother climb the cor-porate ladder and had seen the value that was placed on her mother's achievements outside the home. She had internal-ized her mother's example. At the same time, she appreciated that her father had stayed home with her and her siblings and provided them with wonderful, creative experiences. His con-tribution to the family did not receive the high praise that her mother's did. Joanie was very conflicted, but never wavered regarding the priority she placed on her children's wellbeing.

Within a month of making these changes, Mark's behavior had markedly improved. He presented as a happy, relaxed, intelligent child and his aggressive behaviors disappeared. Come to find out, Mark likes his new little brother. He did miss his preschool teacher, but was allowed to drop by to visit her periodically. Joanie poured herself into raising her children with the same or more passion than she brought to her job and school. She quickly figured out a healthy balance which allowed them to have restful days of just hanging out together and exciting days of field trips and play dates. She also has continued working with Mark on skills that will prepare him for Kindergarten. Joanie and Jim had to cut their household budget down to bare bones, but they understand that this season in their lives is not forever and that they are making the best possible investment in their family.

As things settled out, we began to address this couple's relational issues more directly. Joanie still found herself criticizing Jim and feeling resentful toward him over very small infractions – such as working on the lawn instead of inside the house, or not realizing that she needed him to do something with the children. Jim resented this criticism and felt that nothing he did was ever good enough. Neither one felt that they were loved by the other. Given that the level of negativity did not match up with the severity of the perceived infractions, we backed things up to their families of origin.

Joanie and Jim each took a good hard look at themselves. Joanie realized that she was sounding more and more like her own mother, who criticized her father incessantly. Her father never seemed to do enough to please her mother. Jim realized that his childhood with a mentally ill mother who became increasingly distant and lost in her illness as he grew up, and a father who was often less than loving in his attitude and behavior, had left him insecure and overly sensitive to criticism as he was trying to figure out how to be a husband and father. Once this young couple realized that their negative feelings were less about each other and more about themselves, and that the consequences of a divorce would do serious damage to their precious children, they began to focus on creating a loving environment in their home. They re-focused on the positives in each other and decided to consciously overlook each other's shortcomings. Their communication increased and improved.

Jim described a scene that had played out in their home one evening which said it all. He had come inside and found Joanie and Mark cuddling on the bed. He sat on the edge of the bed to get something out of a drawer and instinctively lay over and put his head on Joanie's lap. He caught Mark's expression at that moment. He described it as a smile that said "Daddy loves Mommy too!" Joanie described the resentments within her as just melting away as she submitted her will to God. She gives God the credit for changing her heart toward Jim. With God's help, this couple beat the odds by surrendering their wills to God and putting the needs of their children before their own. Their two little boys' futures have been transformed because of their parents' sacrificial love for them. This is how it is supposed to be!

****

The culture's approach to meeting needs and finding fulfillment and purpose is entirely backwards and upside down. We are taught to look out for number one and to put our own happiness ahead of the well-being of others, even in our own families. As stated earlier, I cannot count the number of times a parent sitting in my office has said, "You can't expect me to stay in this marriage and continue to be unhappy?" My answer to that is yes, I do expect parents to sacrifice their happiness, if necessary, for the sake of the lives of their children. Abusive situations are the exception. Abuse must never be tolerated. However, unhappiness is a condition that our culture tends to run from, rather than figuring out the source and working through it. The Bible gives the true path to the purpose and fulfillment that all of us desperately seek and it does not come from putting our own wants and desires above others. It is in giving that we are blessed.[70] True love, as we so often hear quoted at wedding ceremonies but few actually experience in a lifetime, is described in First Corinthians 13:4-7 and bears repetition here:

> "Love is patient, love is kind. It does not envy, it does not boast, it is not proud. It is not rude, it is not self-seeking, it is not easily angered, it keeps no record of wrongs. Love does not delight in evil but rejoices with the truth. It always protects, always trusts, always hopes, always perseveres."[71]

I'm speaking to men and women alike. When have we experienced this type of love and, more importantly, when have we given this type of love? How many of us can say we have shown this biblical love to our families? This love is sacrificial. We all desire to be loved in this way but very few of us are interested in extending this type of love to another. When we refuse to give something until we receive it, it is not unconditional. Unconditional love is given when the person we are giving it to does not deserve it or return it.

The most poignant example of sacrificial love that I have heard in recent years is the story of a family in our town. Twenty years ago, doctors discovered that the expectant mother had advanced cancer. The intensive treatment required to save her life would have most likely killed the baby, so the doctors recommended she abort the baby and save herself. She refused to abort the baby and refused treatment, sacrificing her own life so that her child could live. Immediately after giving birth, the mother was taken to another part of the hospital where she passed away within days. This woman gave the ultimate gift of life! This is also the ultimate expression of love that a human being can give. The father remarried and the baby is now a twenty-year-old young man. What a beautiful reunion he will have with his mother someday! Parents frequently say: "I would do anything for my children." Oh really? The sad truth, which is demonstrated by the divorce rate, is that most parents are more concerned with their own happiness than with the life-long consequences their decisions will have on their precious children.

****

So many of us struggle our entire lives with personal insecurities as we chase after our own selfish wants and desires. Perhaps focusing on and chasing after our own desires actually leads to personal unhappiness as we leave our children wounded in the wake of our self-serving lifestyles. Perhaps focusing on giving to others what we wish to receive ourselves is the key. Matthew 7:12 says: "So in everything, do to others what you would have them do to you, for this sums up the Law and the Prophets."[72]

If you are at a point in your life where you realize that you have bought the lies of the culture regarding love and happiness, and you are ready to take a completely different approach to finding fulfillment, I strongly recommend that you read *The Purpose Driven Life* by Rick Warren. His book has been a best seller for years which speaks to the extent of the disillusionment being experienced in our culture. The first sentence of his book states: "It's not about you."[73] What a radical statement in a self-centered world.

If satisfying the desires of the flesh was the answer, our culture would be the happiest, most fulfilled culture that ever set foot on the planet and I would be out of work. We owe it to our children and grandchildren to get our priorities straight and to model the sacrificial love described in the Bible. This means saying no to what our flesh wants to do and yes to what we know is best for our children and families, even if it causes us temporary discomfort or unhappiness. Ultimately, this way of life is the only way to deep fulfillment, sense of purpose, and few regrets. Our children are looking to us to show them the correct way to find personal fulfillment, not the same old same old they see in the culture at large.

****

The following article appeared online in a Huffington Post blog and was written by an anonymous mother expressing her regrets as she looked back over her life. She makes my point much better than I ever could.

I Wish I Could Go Back. . .
Confessions of a Divorced Mom[74]

"If I had a second chance, I would have quit my job when my children were born. I would have not made so many excuses to say, 'I have to work.' Because they were mostly lies. Lies told, because honestly, the weeks I did spend at home scared me to death. It was easier to hire someone to mother them, and pay her to do my job.

I would have not made excuses for only nursing my babies for a few months. I would have told my husband and my friends and my mother-in-law that I would raise my children. The heck with what they 'wanted' or 'expected' or thought I should do. My mother-in-law, although very nasty about the fact that I 'worked,' was more than happy to take my kids on weekends, when I was more than happy to be 'so tired' to raise them myself. My husband and I broke up anyway, as our lives diverged, and without family time to hold us together, we were just spending money, and making excuses for not being with our children.

But I was too obsessed with 'my life' and how I thought I was supposed to live it. Make money, have fun, be everything to all people, except those who really should mean the most to me. I was selfish, and self-absorbed. I wish I could go back and make the difference when it counts.

Now my children have no time for me. At first I was angry, but I understand. I always made excuses as to why I never had time for them. Or took them on a few errands and told people we were taking quality time. All BS. It was about me then.

Now it's too late. They have their own lives, and as my ex and I 'worked' all the time, our children learned to get comfort elsewhere. They expect us to pay for school, which we are doing, and to lend them money, which we do, but it is an artifact of our poor self-absorbed parenting that we feel we have to give them things and money, instead of giving them our time, when we had the chance.

I wish I could change the past. I'd have my children, say the heck with the huge house, and the big screen TV, and the new car every few years, and the vacations, the expensive food, the eating out, the business suits I thought I 'needed,' the radical shoes, the thought that I 'needed' lunch out every day, and the cost of day care. None of which was necessary. I would stop all the excuses, say 'NO' to spending money on anything but the essentials, forget the BS that I 'deserved' what I earned for myself, and spend my time at home and *being* with my children.

Now, their only concerns are what my ex and I can do for them. And, I realize they do this because we bought what we thought was love for too long. I hope they can be there for their children, but I am afraid the pattern will continue.

So, as we move forward, we continue to open the check-book instead of our hearts." - Anonymous

SECTION TWO

AN APPROPRIATE RESPONSE TO THE CULTURAL TSUNAMI

CHAPTER 7

WHERE DO I START?

Typically, when we talk about preparing our children to make healthy decisions about any subject, we assume it's all about education. Most of us believe that if we make sure our kids know all about a particular subject and the dangers involved, they will take in that information and make the right decisions. I agree that education and allowing our children to ask any questions they have is very important at all stages of the parent/child relationship. However, if we believe that education is all that is required of us to be effective guides in the realm of sexuality or drugs and alcohol, it's a little like telling our child how to row a boat, explaining the dangers of Niagara Falls, then putting them in a small rowboat and launching them over the Falls. If we decide to wait until they have a social life and just deal with the issues as they come, it's like paddling that small rowboat up to the edge of Niagara Falls then instructing them on how to survive the Falls as they're going over the edge.

Our culture is enamored with sex education and sex is talked about incessantly. We talk and talk and talk about sex to little or no avail except that more and more teens are sexually active! This approach makes no sense to me at all. Maybe I'm missing something, but I have never in my years of counseling come across one person who couldn't figure out for themselves (usually through media exposure or talking with someone on the school bus) how this sex thing is done! One day our daughters went to the local movie store to rent a romantic comedy that was rated PG13. They accidentally picked up the 'unrated version.' Because it wasn't rated, there were no age restrictions for renting it. They started watching this movie and before their eyes were explicit scenes of a couple having sex. If they had any questions about how people do it, their questions were answered in graphic detail with full nudity. So, no matter how carefully you believe you are restricting your child's exposure to sexually explicit media, you have to figure they are going to see or hear about it someway, somehow.

Yes, parents should give their children the facts about sex, especially regarding STD's and birth control. However, with all the emphasis on sex education, how did the teens in our culture become so confused? Could it be that we, as parents, are as much at fault as the culture? Are we sending mixed messages to our kids in a million different ways?

Parents cannot expect school sex education programs alone to be effective in deterring their adolescent from experimenting sexually. Most sex education programs pretend to be values neutral, but are really values negative. If your child is lucky enough to have an abstinence-based sex education program in their school, they are at least presented with the fact that only through abstinence will they be protected from the multitude of negative consequences associated with casual sexual activity. However, if instilling fear were enough to stop people from having sex we would not have the rate of genital herpes that we have today (approximately 30 million, with one million new cases diagnosed each year. 500,000 of those new cases are in the United States.[75]) Once again, the Centers for Disease Control recently released a report stating that one in four teenage girls has or has had a sexually transmitted disease and that many of them were infected soon after their first sexual encounter.[76] Guess what the suggested response to this outrageous statistic was – "renewed calls for better sexual health education."[77] Of course education is important, but education does not create the strength of character in an immature teenager to say no to their flesh and to the *Cultural Tsunami* that pressures them to give in to sexual temptation.

Another aspect of early sex education that we often do not consider is that we are providing explicit sexual information to children who are not emotionally or psychologically ready for that information. There is currently a push to begin explicit sex education as early as Kindergarten. This does not move us toward the supposed goal of preventing early sexual experimentation in children. It robs children of their innocence and only serves to sexualize them. A sexual curiosity is turned on within them that they are not ready to handle. We are forcing children to deal with sexuality at a level for which they are not developmentally prepared, and then we expect them to be mature enough to discern appropriate and inappropriate ways to behave as a result of this knowledge. You may choose to remove your child from school on the days the sex education curriculum is presented; but I can assure you they will hear all about it from their peers in the days following the presentation.

So what can we do when our culture is so permeated with messages promoting sexual immorality? How do we instill in our children the desire and the strength and a good enough reason to say no to sexual immorality and experimentation with drugs and alcohol? We need to ask ourselves what skills, strengths, and knowledge they will need to possess so that they have the power and desire to say no when the temptation and opportunity are right in front of them. It's not enough to educate our children. They must internalize the truth that the prize for exhibiting self-control and saying no to their body now is worth the delayed gratification. I had a young adult single man tell me recently that he is counting on the payoff for remaining sexually pure now to be a lifetime of amazing sex with his future wife. From my experience counseling married couples who are having unsatisfying sexual relations, there is almost always sexual baggage (often incurable STDs) and comparisons to previous sexual relationships or to pornographic images contributing to their current sexual dissatisfaction. I think the odds are in favor of this young man getting the reward he is so patiently awaiting.

****

There are several important core beliefs and character traits that any teenager will need to have to remain sexually pure until marriage and to say no to drugs and alcohol. Here are a few:

- The understanding and belief that when the brain and the emotions/flesh are in conflict, the brain must always override emotions and desires of the flesh. They must develop the habit of checking their desires and emotions against what their brain is telling them.
- The ability and determination to say no to themselves when every fiber of their flesh is saying yes. In other words, delaying or refusing gratification of the flesh, sometimes with no immediate reward for doing so.
- The strength of character to stand alone against the crowd.
- The strength of character to tolerate being teased and ridiculed.
- The strength of character to tolerate negative emotions and feelings of loneliness.
- The ability to project into the future and see the promised land that is awaiting them if they are willing to suffer a little bit now. Knowing the story of Joseph in Genesis and present-day examples will help develop this trait.
- A basic respect for authority, which translates into respect for God.
- A good enough relationship with Mom and Dad to be able to separate and begin making their own decisions in healthy ways. In other words, sex or drugs do not become tools for rebellion.

- An absolute belief that they are capable of withstanding the *Cultural Tsunami* and the desires of their own flesh, to accomplish their long-term goals.

These are some pretty amazing character traits that are not seen in most teenagers today. The unfortunate truth is, these character traits are not seen in a lot of adults today. Just the other day, a single mother expressed to me that she is instilling in her teenage daughter the belief that education is more important than boys and that she is to stay pure until marriage. When I challenged the mother that she needs to do the same, she responded that it was too difficult for her to stay pure. We expect disciplined behavior from our children that we are not willing to expect from ourselves. No wonder so many teenagers are having sex if this is what's required to be able to say no to sexual activity and the adults around them are not living what they profess to believe.

So, how on earth do we instill these traits in our children? First, we must model a life that our children can emulate. We must believe ourselves that it is absolutely possible for our children to possess these character traits and make decisions that go against the mainstream of the culture. And we must engage in diligent, intentional training of our children that sets aside our own emotional needs and desires. We must want our children to live righteous lives more than we desire for them to be popular in high school!

The overriding difference between people who give in to sexual immorality and drug and alcohol use, and people who are strong enough to make counter-cultural decisions, is whether they are making their decisions based on emotion and immediate gratification of the flesh (very short-term thinking) or based on logical reasoning using their brain and basing their decisions on goals and priorities they have already established for their life (long-term, big picture thinking). A person is less likely to have regrets in life if they make decisions based on the big picture and how today's decisions will affect their future goals in life. We have to train our children to see the big picture because living in the moment is what the flesh does naturally.

****

Most of you have probably heard of Nick Vujicic, a man who was born with no arms or legs. He has a ministry called "Life Without Limbs." If you have never heard him speak, you must take a few moments and watch a couple of his YouTube videos. He is incredible!

In his book, *Life Without Limits*, Nick explains how his parents approached his physical limitations when he was a child. As Nick describes it:

> "I was just a toddler when my medical team recommended that my parents put me in a play group with other kids labeled "disabled." Their challenges ranged from missing limbs to cystic fibrosis and severe mental disorders. My parents had great love and empathy for other special needs kids and their families, but they don't think any child should be limited to one group of playmates. They held on to the conviction that my life would have no limits, and they fought to keep that dream alive."[78]

Nick's mother told him:

> "Nicholas, you need to play with normal children because you are normal. You just have a few bits and pieces missing, that's all,"[79]

Nick realizes that his parents set the tone for his entire life by treating him as though he is normal and refusing to put limitations on their expectations for his future. We put limits on our able-bodied children when we treat them as though they cannot handle challenges and disappointments. When we coddle and overprotect our children, run interference for them, defend them from any and all perceived threats and attempt to keep them from experiencing and dealing with challenges, we handicap them emotionally and psychologically. Nick's parents could have educated him at home or in a special school environment. Wanting him to believe in his normalcy, they placed him in a school with able-bodied children.

In *Life Without Limits*, Nick describes being a mere first-grader when he was bullied by a third grade boy. The boy taunted Nick and challenged him to a fight. Nick accepted the challenge. They fought and it ended with Nick giving the boy a bloody nose and the boy running away in tears.[80] Of course, we don't want our children to fight with their peers. However, the truth of the matter is that our children will experience conflict with their peers and authority figures as they grow up. They will experience unfair treatment by peers and adults alike. This world is not fair. We cannot change that. What our children need is for us to train them in appropriate strategies and instill in them the confidence to deal with the unfairness and cruelty of the world without crumbling. The only way they gain that confidence is if we allow them to have negative experiences and to face and work through these experiences. Yes, we are there to coach them through but we must not jump in the middle and run interference every time our child is faced with a challenge. Even if your child has to accept a negative out-come and things don't work out perfectly in the end, your child will learn that he is capable of dealing with a bad situation and surviving intact. If Nick had been segregated into a special needs classroom and overprotected, chances are he would not have the amazing life and ministry he has today. A couple years ago Nick got married and recently became a father.

Nick's parents set a goal for their son – to have a limit-less life – then they set about making decisions that would allow him to develop the qualities he needed to live up to his potential. In the process, they planted a core belief inside of him that he is not handicapped and can do just about anything with enough ingenuity and effort. Isn't that the basic founda-tion of self-esteem? Nick has proven his parents right as he has become adept at skateboarding, swimming, surfing, scuba diving, and many other physical challenges that many able-bodied people are afraid to try.

I would venture to say that many teenagers today have lower self-esteem than this man with no arms and legs. Why is that? Because we treat them like princes and princesses who might melt if they have to suffer a little and are too weak to deal with whatever the culture dishes out. We also act as though it's the end of the world if our children are not happy. This sends the message to them that happiness is the goal and unhappiness is to be avoided by whatever means necessary. We will go into debt to make sure our children have the right clothes and technological devices to fit in and be envied by their peers. Hence, they are given the message that their self-worth is in the eyes of their peers based on material possessions. In other words, they are hot stuff if they have the absolute latest technology and they are losers if they have an old, outdated cell phone. Maybe we think we might fall apart if we have to see our kids suffering a little. We don't want them to be unhappy for a second because, in our twisted culture, an unhappy kid equals bad parenting. It really is all about us and our own insecurities. We fear that someone might think we're bad parents! In my early years as a parent, I had no confidence in my own instincts so I relied on the feedback of others to feel good or bad about myself as a parent.

I often wonder, as well, if many parents have a fear of rejection deep inside of them that originated in their own childhoods. The thought of our own children rejecting us, even in a moment of rebellion, is devastating and churns up intense feelings within us. As a result, we sacrifice our children on the altar of our own feelings and emotional needs. We refuse to stand up and be what our kids need us to be because having our children angry with us causes an emotional crisis within us. If we don't get over ourselves and set aside our own emotions, we will be unable to communicate clear beliefs and expectations to our children and we will continually get in the way of lessons they need to learn.

****

The first four character traits I previously enumerated require a healthy dose of self-esteem. So how do we develop self-esteem in our children? It comes down to our expectations of what they are capable of. Coddling our kids sends a clear message about our expectations – they are too weak to handle the challenges of life. We, the parents, instill core beliefs into the depths of our children from the time they are born. Our feedback, behavior, and expectations of them send clear messages that settle into their soul.

We've discussed the vulnerability and self-doubt that exists in many teenage girls, but what about the boys? The boys I meet with in my office have not been challenged in life to really see what they are made of. Parents typically give their sons nice little chores around the house like taking out the trash and loading the dishwasher. It is a given that boys and girls need to be expected to do chores around the house. No chore should be seen as exclusively male or female. If your kids are not participating in keeping the household running, you need to go back to square one. Unfortunately, we often stop there and think doing chores around the house is a lot to ask of our kids. If they do their chores regularly without too much grief, we pat ourselves on the back and think we've done our job as parents. The most challenging activity boys are typically given responsibility for in our culture is to master a lawn mower, and even then if the lawn mower breaks down they often have no clue what to do about it. What are we communicating to our sons about our expectations of them when we only allow them to be challenged in very controlled, protected situations?

Boys are wired differently. They are the risk takers and protectors. They need an adrenaline rush on a regular basis. They need a significant purpose and challenge in life. Of course, there are quiet, studious boys who get their excitement from studying physics and don't need the excitement of testing out their theories. In the same way, there are girls who are wired more like boys in the risk taking, living on the

127

edge department. I'm speaking in generalities here; however, I have come to believe that, in the same way that vulnerable girls look for feelings of personal worth through sexual activity, our sons are looking for what's missing in their lives when they engage in self-destructive behaviors. Experimenting with drugs is one of the most readily-available, risk taking, living on the edge behaviors that our boys have available to them (remember the story of Bobby?). Some young men go as far as selling drugs and carrying guns and knives to get this adrenaline rush. There are not many appropriate living on the edge, risk taking opportunities available to teenagers in our culture. Organized sports are our best attempt at meeting this need in kids and teenagers. They serve the important purpose of giving teenagers of both sex an outlet for competition and physical challenge, but they are often SO organized. Where's the risk and living on the edge excitement when you're being driven to practices by Mom, who makes sure you have your mouth guard, shin guards, padding, uniform, and proper shoes, then sits in the stands smiling and cheering you on as you carefully obey every rule that is intended to keep you from getting hurt? Even some of our best young athletes are engaging in dangerous, risky behaviors on the side. Our young men, and many of our young women, are bored!

****

The Boy Scouts of America does a very good job of providing opportunities for boys to challenge themselves and test their limits (Girl Scouts does the same for girls). I personally know three young men who have recently achieved the level of Eagle Scout. They are confident and fearless. One of them told me that they frequently see younger boys drop out of scouting as soon as it gets tough. Parents are often quick to allow them to quit because they are worried about their sons being lonely or scared or miserable on long hikes or the parents are afraid their child might get hurt. Some parents are just too busy with other things to invest the time and effort into supporting their child's involvement in the scouting program. When we really believe in our sons, we will push them beyond their perceived limits and fears and desire for them to reach their full potential.

A columnist named Lenore Skenazy has been labeled by some as "America's worst mom"[81]in response to an article she wrote which she expanded into a book she titled *Free-Range Kids: Giving Our Children the Freedom We Had Without Going Nuts.*[82] Her message is that we need to give our children longer leashes and less fear-driven lives. She believes that the world has not become more dangerous but that our society has become fearful of "even very tiny risks."[83] I don't know if I would agree with everything she proposes, but I do believe she has an important point that is worth serious consideration.

****

Dr. Ben Carson, the world-renowned neurosurgeon at Johns Hopkins Medical Center, recently wrote a book called *Take the Risk*. He talks about how risk averse our society has become, in some cases to our detriment. His words are enlightening:

> "In our culture, security has become an obsession. It dictates everything from public policy to Madison Avenue's commercial appeals, from medical care to education and personal and family life. We buy every kind of insurance. . . we pay extra for warranties. . . We purchase safety seats to keep our children secure and safety helmets for them to wear on their bike rides around the block. . . What we're buying and what everyone is selling us is the promise of "security." And yet the only thing we can be sure of is that someday every one of us will die."[84]

So, if young men are wired to need the excitement of risk taking, where are they going to find an outlet for that need in an appropriate way in our society? Dr. Carson addressed the lack of logical balance in our culture after being asked to make the recommendation that children wear helmets when riding tricycles. Dr. Carson's opinions come from the perspective of someone who has seen severe injuries in young people:

> "I've seen enough tragic head trauma in my career that I don't thoughtlessly dismiss the argument of those who say, "If we could prevent one child from suffering, we should." But where do we stop? More kids probably come into ERs every year with head injuries from falling off beds than off trikes. Do we next recommend children wear helmets when they sleep? While we're at it, why not recommend they wear goggles to prevent something from getting in their eyes? Maybe just order them little yellow bio-hazard suits to protect them from everything. But that might make it harder to ride tricycles without catching the pant legs in the spokes and risking a tear in the suit or a dangerous fall. On and on it goes. . ."[85]

Beyond the issue of physical risk is our aversion as parents to allowing our children to experience emotional risks. Have you heard the term 'helicopter parents?' It was coined to describe the hovering that more and more parents are doing in an attempt to protect their children from disappointment or hardship or unfairness of any kind. There's even an online quiz you can take to determine if you are a helicopter parent.[86] More and more helicopter parents are continuing this behavior into the college years. University deans are increasingly required to deal with phone calls from parents concerned about their children who are away at college.

When you read Dr. Carson's personal story of his own upbringing, you clearly see that he learned appropriate risk-taking and fearlessness through personal experiences. His mother was too focused on survival to spend time coddling her two sons. These risk-taking skills have enabled him to become the neurosurgeon that he is today, taking on challenging surgeries that other surgeons often refuse to perform. Our world needs 'Dr. Carsons' to rise up from this generation of teenagers. We need to stop over-protecting our children and give them opportunities to push their limits if there is any hope of this generation developing men and women who struggle through challenges, instead of looking for an escape.

Dr. Carson was not raised in a privileged environment by parents who were professionals themselves. He was raised by a single mother who could not read. She was married at 13 and, when her husband left, it took all she had in her to provide the very basics for her two sons. Dr. Carson grew up in the inner-cities of Detroit and Boston.

A major turning point in his life was when he decided in 5th grade that he wanted to be a doctor. He had heard about medical missionaries in church and wanted to help people. In spite of their situation and his poor academic performance in school, his mother looked him in the eyes and said "Listen to me Benny. If you ask the Lord for something and believe he will do it, then it'll happen."[87] She had high expectations for her sons and believed they could achieve them, in spite of their circumstances.

One day Dr. Carson's mother sat him and his brother, Curtis, down to discuss their failing grades in school. She told them she was going to ask God what to do. The next morning she told them that God revealed to her that they were watching too much TV and not studying enough. She set a limit of 3 TV shows per week. They argued with her but she stood her ground. Then she said they had to read two books each week of their own choosing and write a report on each. She had them read their reports to her each week. They didn't realize at the time that she couldn't read them herself.

Dr. Carson remembers the response from parents in the neighborhood to these new restrictions:

"Curtis and I weren't the only ones to question whether she heard the Lord right. Even some of her friends, other mothers, told her she was being too hard on us, that boys needed time outside to play. Some people actually warned Mother she would risk making us hate her for demanding we turn off the TV to read books and write reports."[88]

Dr. Carson describes the results of his mother's bold parenting:

"In two years of disciplined, weekly reading, I went from the absolute bottom of my class to the top – in almost every subject. Mother was thrilled. No longer was I at risk for failing out of school, and I was more convinced than ever that I was going to be a doctor."[89]

When Dr. Carson was accepted into Yale, he said he had "achieved at a level beyond all expectations – except those of my mother and myself."[90] There is so much we can learn from this uneducated, African-American single mother who only had the Lord to turn to when she didn't know what else to do. When she made a decision about a course of action, she was unflinching in her determination. It didn't matter to her if everyone on Earth disagreed with her convictions. And when she told her two boys to do something, she fully expected them to do it. She commanded their respect. Wow!

We have become so over-educated and insecure within ourselves, that we often don't even know how to make a deci-sion and require our children to do something that they might not want to do. We project our own insecurities and fears onto our children and deep-down believe that they can't handle disappointment and challenges. What an insult to them! It's no wonder our kids take drastic measures to separate from us. Then there are those who don't have the will to separate from their hovering parents. They make up the recent phenomenon of "boomerang" kids who move back in with their parents after attempting or even graduating college or briefly living on their own.[91] Some young people never leave in the first place, allowing their parents to take care of them indefinitely. Of course, many of them are enjoying active sex lives with girlfriends or boyfriends living with them or sleeping with them under Mom and Dad's roof.

****

My sister, Kimberly and her husband Michael have 5 children – 4 boys and one girl. Michael builds and fixes things himself, and is a retired Army Staff Sargent. He expects his sons to work alongside him when he has a project going, which is most of the time. I will never forget when they were being transferred to a different Army base and were preparing to put their townhouse on the market. Michael had their 11-year old son Benjamin on the roof with him helping him re-roof the house. He had the two next oldest boys, Adam and Matthew, carrying shingles and tools for them. They have built so many projects together. Michael challenges his boys and if Kimberly is afraid they might get hurt, she keeps it to herself and allows Michael to be the dad. Their sons are fearless and confident. When Michael has been deployed for long periods of time, the older boys step up and do whatever Kimberly needs them to do. It's expected of them. These boys have been challenged physically and emotionally and their parents aren't afraid to allow them to take appropriate risks.

Michael and Kimberly have lived in many different places, both overseas and in the States, and the kids have been required to leave behind friends and adapt to new people and places every 3-4 years. Kimberly homeschools them so that their education is consistent, and they always find a church and/or homeschool group to get involved in. As if having 5 kids and homeschooling weren't enough, Kimberly takes a couple of the kids every week and does meals-on-wheels deliveries. She and the children also help clean the church building every week. They could feel sorry for their kids and focus on how difficult their military lifestyle is at times. They could coddle their children to help make up for the frequent moves and the fact that they have missed out on some of the experiences that American teenagers take for granted. They don't. Every day they get down to business, focus on what needs to get done, and expect their kids to rise to the occasion.

****

As Christians, we know that God only expects us to do what we can in any given moment and that we can trust Him to take it from there. However, God does expect us to sacrificially fight for our children, even if it means driving to that party and embarrassing our teenager and ourselves in front of everyone to put them in the car and bring them home.

My best advice to parents of teenagers who are already involved in the party scene is to do absolutely everything you can do to get in the way of their drug or alcohol use. You have every right to search their bedroom if you have any suspicion of drug or alcohol use. Take away the car keys if you need to and restrict them from going to friends' houses. Put them on lock-down in your home only allowing them to go to school, if need be. If the school is the problem, do what you have to do to change schools or have them placed on homebound schooling or into online schooling from home. You may need to get law enforcement involved if there is ongoing drug abuse. If need be, put your child into a drug treatment center. Do absolutely everything you can do while your child is still a minor. If your child becomes violent or threatens violence, it's time to take drastic measures and place them in a facility before someone in the home gets hurt or your teenager ends up in jail or dead. If your adult child is an addict and refuses to get help, you must separate them from the family. Do not allow them to live in your home and do not allow their drug abuse to destroy the rest of the family, especially their siblings. Follow the example of the father in the biblical story of the Prodigal Son (see Chapter 15). Be ready to welcome them home and help them any way you can when they decide to deal with their addiction but not while they are still using.

CHAPTER 8

WHAT DO YOU EXPECT FROM YOUR TEENAGER?

My experience with parents of children and teenagers in the American culture is that most parents expect very little from their children in the realm of self-control. Many parents today are content if their teenagers get to adulthood without unwanted pregnancies or getting arrested. Unfortunately, many of our teenagers are rising, or should I say sinking, to that level of expectation.

Based on my own experiences with adolescents and their parents over the past 15 years, I have yet to run into a Christian parent who expresses that they want their child to become sexually active as a teenager. For Christians, we would ideally prefer that our children wait until their wedding night to give themselves totally to the person who has just committed his or her life to them before God. Besides the obvious moral implications, the older we get the more we become aware of the dangers of reckless sexual activity. Look at what happened to Laura, and her behavior would not even be considered reckless by the world's standards.

Unfortunately, many parents take the approach they see on television where the concerned TV parent, in a heartfelt moment, tells their teen to wait for their first sexual encounter until they meet that "special someone" or until they know they are "ready" (whatever that means!). That kind of a vague approach confuses children more than it helps them. But it lets parents off the hook because only the teenager knows how he or she feels. It also tells teenagers that the decisions they make about sexual activity are to be based on emotions, rather than on clear, reasonable thinking that originates in the brain.

We must boldly set clear goals and expectations for our children – the higher the better! If we don't believe they can achieve the goal of abstinence, why will they believe they can do it? Believe it or not, there are young people today who remain abstinent until they are married. The Jonas Brothers and Jordin Sparks brought purity rings into the public con- sciousness. Actually, Rebecca St. James, who is an award- winning Christian songwriter and recording artist, has been encouraging teenagers and young adults to remain sexually pure until marriage since she was a teenager herself.

If sexual immorality is so dangerous on so many levels, and makes it almost impossible to experience the ultimate, deeply satisfying intimate sexual relationship with the one person we will spend the rest of our lives with, why are we as parents failing so miserably in conveying the importance of abstinence to our teenagers? I have encountered many parents who have thrown up their hands and believe that teenage sexual activity is just a natural occurrence to be expected. They have convinced themselves that it is not a big deal. Could it be that we, ourselves, have ambiguous feelings about sex and don't really buy into the importance of sexual purity? Are we numbed by a culture that is entertained by "Sex and the City" and other popular television shows that depict casual sex as something everyone engages in with very few consequences? Are we, the parents, struggling with these very issues in our own personal lives?

If there are any of you who doubt whether your teenager is capable of rising to high standards, I think it might be helpful to revisit the true story of a young man named Joseph, whose life is described in the Bible in chapters 37-50 in the book of

Genesis. If you're not familiar with Joseph, it's the same story depicted in the Broadway musical "Joseph and the Amazing, Technicolor Dreamcoat." I'm going to paraphrase parts of the story so I encourage you to pick up your Bible and read it in its entirety.

Joseph was no different than any other young man as far as sexual temptation and desire. He faced a particularly bold attempt at sexual seduction and overcame with his purity intact. Young Joseph was "well built and handsome."[92] He was a slave in the home of Potiphar. He was so determined that he was going to stay sexually pure that when Potiphar's wife attempted to seduce him day after day, he said to her "How could I do such a wicked thing and sin against God?"[93] Joseph refused to even be around her, but Potiphar's wife was determined to have him. She had tried and tried to talk him into sleeping with her and it hadn't worked, so she arranged to be alone in the house with him one day. She grabbed his cloak, demanding that he come to bed with her. Joseph left his cloak in her hand and ran out of the house naked rather than give in to sexual sin. How many young men today would go to that length to avoid sexual sin? Joseph actually ended up imprisoned as a result of this encounter because Potiphar's wife claimed that he tried to rape her and had run away when she yelled. It was her word against his and he was a mere slave.

After enduring this and many other hardships and passing many tests, Joseph miraculously ended up ruling over Egypt and being used by God to save many lives. He also ended up enjoying the pleasures of intimacy in a marriage relationship. In retrospect, we can clearly see that if Joseph had given in to Potiphar's wife and indulged in physical pleasures at that time, he would have left the righteous path God had for him that ultimately led to him ruling over Egypt.

Joseph could have rationalized giving in to sexual immorality in many ways. After all, how could he be expected to say no to his master's wife when she had the power to have him thrown into prison? He was a mere slave. Wasn't he supposed to obey his master's wife? He knew no one would believe his side of the story if he rejected her and made her angry. His reputation would be ruined as he sat in prison and as she continued to tell lies about him. How could that possibly be God's will for him? Also, come on! God understands how difficult it is for a young man with intense sexual urges to say no to a beautiful woman throwing herself at him! Plus, God will forgive us for our shortcomings. So, what's the harm? No one's perfect. I've heard similar rationalizations from teenage clients in my office who can't understand why or how they are expected to say no to sex. I also frequently encounter adults with similar rationalizations for sexual immorality who can't understand why their lives and relationships are off-track and unfulfilling.

We have before us in the life of Joseph a beautiful example of the rewards of righteous living in the face of confusing twists and turns which, at the time, made no sense at all. The challenges Joseph experienced seemed harsh and unfair, especially given his faithfulness to God. Joseph's determination to obey God and remain pure before God, no matter what the cost, was tested time and again before he was put in the position of blessing and responsibility God had for him. Another very important part of the story of Joseph is that "while Joseph was there in prison the Lord was with him; he showed him kindness and granted him favor. . ."[94] When our teenagers determine to follow the path of sexual purity, no matter what the cost, God is with them showing them kindness and granting them favor, even in the face of persecution. We must be more concerned with and more focused on our children's relationship with God as opposed to their level of popularity with their peers, and we must diligently train them from a young age to live out that same priority.

****

Yes, God forgives us when we fail to meet His standards, but there are repercussions for our sinful indulgences that we are sometimes unaware of or don't realize are connected to our choices. Jeremiah 29:11 says "For I know the plans I have for you, declares the Lord. Plans to prosper you and not to harm you, plans to give you hope and a future."[95] The story of the life of Joseph demonstrates the power of a righteous life in the face of confusion, unfair treatment, and circumstances that seem hopeless. God tells us that He is the same "yesterday and today and forever."[96] God is the same now as when He was guiding Joseph's life. He has a plan for every one of us but He gave us a free will to decide for ourselves whether we want His plan or our own plan. As parents, our goal needs to be instilling the determination of Joseph into our children. This level of determination is required to withstand the testing and temptation that comes along and threatens to steal the ultimate blessings God has planned and prepared for them.

So when Joseph, at age 30, finally reached the pinnacle of God's plan for him, do you think he sat on his throne in Egypt and thought, "Man, I wish I had slept with Potiphar's wife when I had the chance! She was hot!" Joseph's attitude regarding all that had happened to him is revealed when he tells his brothers "You intended to harm me, but God intended it for good to accomplish what is now being done, the saving of many lives."[97] Joseph understood that there was a purpose in all the suffering he experienced at the hands of others and that, because he remained obedient to God through it all, God's ultimate plan came about. Joseph was vindicated and Joseph's brothers, who started all the craziness in Joseph's life, were required to bow before Joseph and beg for the provisions they needed for their very survival and the survival of their families. Joseph is one of my favorite people in the Bible!

****

Now, back to the present day. For Christians, we would ideally prefer that our children wait until their wedding night to give themselves totally to the person who has just committed his or her life to them before God. Also, we would ideally prefer that our children stay away from drugs and alcohol.

Do you really believe it is possible for your child to have the determination of Joseph regarding sexual behavior and drug and alcohol use? Do you really believe it's possible for any teenager today to be that strong or do you think this story in the Bible is just a nice little story that has no relevance in the 21st century? Do you send your children the clear message, with no doubt on your face or in your voice, that it is the right thing to do and that you fully expect and believe that they will wait until they are married to have sex and that they will avoid drug and alcohol use? Or do you backpedal and remind your children (and yourself) that God is a forgiving God so if they can't wait, just be sure to use a condom and be careful when choosing their sexual partners? Regarding drugs and alcohol, do you just hope against hope that your teenager will not drive under the influence and will call you if they end up impaired at someone else's house? Or, do you avoid these difficult subjects altogether and just hope for the best?

Even more importantly, what are you modeling for your children? Do you tell them to remain sexually pure while, at the same time, you have a live-in boyfriend or girlfriend? Do you have sleepovers with a boyfriend or girlfriend and think you are hiding it from your children? Do you have a well-stocked liquor cabinet and do your children see you getting tipsy or drunk on occasion, while at the same time warning them of the dangers of alcohol? Your words only have meaning if they are backed up by your actions. Every day of your lives you are demonstrating to your children how to live. If you truly desire to do whatever it takes to give your child the best possible chance to live a godly life, with as little baggage and regret as possible, you must put your complete faith in God. You must believe that by His grace and with His help it is possible for your child to abstain from experimentation with sex, drugs and alcohol. You must also believe this for your own life, and demonstrate that belief before your children.

If you are not living a life that sets that example for your children, it's never too late to confess your sinful choices to God and to your children and repent. Commit yourself today, with God's help, to begin living a life of obedience to God. Even if your spouse isn't following God, you alone can set the example and you will, as a result, see a change in your children. Their respect for you will increase and you will be able to challenge them, with credibility, to do the same.

CHAPTER 9

TRAIN UP A CHILD

My first real eye-opening experience with adolescence was in my own home when our oldest child, Chris, entered 6th grade in a large public middle school. I had been a stay-at-home mom since Chris was born and any experience I had with children in general up to that point was with pre-adolescents the same ages as my children. At this time, our daughter, Becca, was 9-years-old and our twins, Michelle and Heather, were 2-years-old.

Chris was, and is, an amazing, extremely strong-willed, intelligent, handsome, outgoing kid who had run circles around his Dad and I since he could run. However, until adolescence, we could work around any issues we had with him and most of the time his behavior stayed within acceptable boundaries. In Chris's world, up until that time, the options were pretty limited for getting into real mischief and his Dad and I looked at him through rose-colored glasses. We did not set immovable limits in the smaller things because those smaller things didn't seem like such a big deal at the time. What a rude awakening we had ahead of us!

I have spoken with many parents who have had a similar experience. They will say "Johnny gave me no trouble at all" until that magical day little Johnny hit adolescence. We tend to blame the stage of adolescence when really the defiance we are experiencing at age 12 usually began in toddlerhood and had plenty of opportunity to grow and flourish by the time they hit adolescence. As young parents, my husband and I had neglected to set firm, immovable, consistent boundaries with our first two children and we had rarely allowed them to experience disappointment. Becca's temperament was the polar opposite of Chris's. She was compliant, quiet, shy, sensitive and boundlessly sweet. My experience, both personal and professional, bears out the truth of Dr. James Dobson's explanation of temperaments in his book and workbook, *The New Strong-Willed Child.*[98] He believes that children are born with a temperament that falls somewhere on a continuum between the extremes of strong-willed and compliant. Dr. Dobson admits to a change in his original conclusion that the continuum looks like a bell curve with a few kids at the temperamental extremes and most kids falling somewhere in the middle. Admitting that his conclusions in this regard are not based on a scientific study but on his own interactions with over 100,000 parents, he now believes that the overwhelming majority of children are born with a strong-willed temperament. My personal and professional experiences support that conclusion.

For almost 7 years, Chris and Becca were our only two children. Dr. Dobson describes Chris and Becca to a tee when he states that "In a family with two children, one is likely to be compliant and the other defiant. . . . There they are, born to the same parents, but as different as if they came from different planets."[99] Like most young parents, we absolutely abhorred seeing our children hurt or disappointed in any way and, conversely, we absolutely delighted in seeing our children's dreams come true. How on earth could this possibly add up to bad parenting? Weren't our hearts in the right place?

I'm sure you can see what was coming when a strong-willed, intelligent kid like Chris, who had been treated at home as though the universe revolved around him, hit 6th grade and the *Cultural Tsunami* hit him. I will not go into specifics about Chris's life out of respect for his privacy; however, there were years of struggle and heartache ahead for him and our family.

He is now, at age 30, professionally successful and happily married to a wonderful young woman. One of the saddest side effects of rebellion within a family is the effect it has on the lives of the siblings. Rebecca, Michelle and Heather could write a book about their personal experiences during the years of Chris's rebellious living. They came through it having learned a lot and they love their brother.

If you're wondering how the girls turned out, Rebecca is happily married to a wonderful young man and is a Licensed Professional Counselor. We give her all the credit for her successes, which are many. Our twin daughters, Michelle and Heather, graduated from Bible College. Heather is a missionary in Africa and Michelle is pursuing further education. Someone recently said to me "You are obviously an amazing mother. Look how your kids turned out." I quickly corrected her. No, I am not an amazing mother. I'm a very average mother who tried to do the best I knew how to do, just like most of the mothers reading this book. If there was one thing that I know I did right, it was submitting to God in my own life as I was raising my children. That submission allowed God to work in my life and in my children's lives. God's grace and my children themselves get the credit for their successes in life.

For many Christian parents, there are two basic verses from the Bible that they can quote in reference to parenting, and often those verses are plucked from the Bible and referred to completely out of context. Remember this one: "Train a child in the way he should go, and when he is old he will not turn from it."[100] This verse is often quoted in an effort to reassure parents that God has promised that their wayward child will return to the faith. However, the book of Proverbs is filled with God's wisdom, not God's promises, as explained in the first chapter. The book of Proverbs is the bounty of God's wisdom applied to human nature. If we live by the teachings of Proverbs, we will have fulfilling relationships and godly character, and will avoid many painful pitfalls in life. Proverbs gives us a very good understanding of human nature that we can apply to any situation, especially parenting.

We, as parents, often interpret Proverbs 22:6 to mean that if we teach our children right from wrong and take them to church, we are guaranteed that, even if they stray during their teen or young adult years, they will return to God and the church and, before long, we will be vindicated as good parents after all! Sometimes I wish that WAS a promise from God, but think about what that would mean. If it was a promise, it would mean that our free will as individuals is taken away from us and we would be locked into turning out the way our parents raised us to be. Each individual has the freedom to decide his or her own path. Kids who grow up in loving, Christian homes with intentional training have a distinct foundational advantage in life that makes it much more likely they will come back to the narrow path that leads to life when they are adults.

The NET Bible includes 60,932 translation notes and is a very helpful online tool for understanding the various translations of a particular passage.[101] As the NET Bible translation notes explain this verse: "proverbs are not universal truths. One can anticipate positive results from careful child-training – but there may be an occasional exception."[102]

There are two ways that Bible scholars have looked at this passage, and I believe that both perspectives offer insights that can be helpful to parents. That's the beauty of Scripture. The same verse can speak truth to us in different ways. The importance of this verse in the lives of Christian parents is summed up by James-Michael Smith in an online article entitled "Train up a child?" He says:

"If you ask new moms and dads what their favorite Bible verse is, chances are they'll rattle off Proverbs 22:6 without hesitation. However, for many parents, Prov. 22:6 later becomes their least favorite verse in Scripture due to their children growing up and leaving the faith they tried so hard to instill in them through all those years of bedtime prayers, VBS activities, Sunday School lessons and youth group gatherings."[103]

How true! James-Michael Smith, in the same article, goes on to present the converse interpretation of Proverbs 22:6 to be: "If you spoil your child, don't expect anything other than a spoiled adult to be the result."[104] Of course, I think we can all agree that there is truth in that statement.

The NET Bible Translation Notes for Proverbs 22:6 offer a clear summation of this verse:

> "In the book of Proverbs there are only two ways that a person can go, the way of the wise or righteousness, and the way of the fool. One takes training, and the other does not."[105]

What does this mean in everyday language? Guidance and intervention of some kind are usually required for us to choose the narrow path that leads to life, as described in Matthew 7:14 (see below). However, it requires no training at all for a person to develop self-centered qualities. Any parent with a toddler knows this first hand. It is the extremely rare child who naturally, without intervention, desires to share his/her toys and runs around saying "yes" to whatever his/her mother or father tells him to do. Overly-compliant children are typically people-pleasers and are finding other, more subtle ways to get what they want. Usually they aren't really submitting to authority in their spirit. The character traits of cooperation and sharing are instilled through parental guidance and training.

The wide gate and broad road referred to in Matthew 7:14 represent the natural, easy way to flow with the culture in this life. Jesus said:

> "Enter through the narrow gate. For wide is the gate and broad is the road that leads to destruction, and many enter through it. But small is the gate and narrow the road that leads to life and only a few find it."[106]

The *Cultural Tsunami* leads right through the wide gate down the broad road to destruction. Bobby and Laura, in our earlier examples, got caught up in the tsunami and carried away. Their lives, as they were given to them by God, were greatly damaged. Only God Himself, through his mercy and grace, can and will redeem their lives if they surrender to Him. But they will still have to live with many of the consequences of their actions. It takes a deliberate, consistent, determined effort to enter through the small gate and stay on the narrow road that leads to life. That's why only a few find it and remain on it. It takes deliberate training on the part of parents to develop the desire and the strength in our children to follow that narrow road. There are people who grow up in non-Christian homes and still choose to follow the Lord, but we are more likely to follow the path we are taught as children (see stats supporting this on the next page).

So, there are two points to be made in these translations of Proverbs 22:6. One, it takes training to lead a child down the right, godly path in life. The second point is that the way a child is trained as he is growing up is most likely the path he will come back to in adulthood. If you train (or allow) a child to remain unchallenged in the self-centered state they were born in, he/she will most likely develop into an extremely self-centered adult. We've all met these over-indulged children in adult bodies! However, if you deliberately train a child to be godly, they will most likely be drawn back to a godly way of life in adulthood. These are words of wisdom from God for us to remember as parents. Now there is that thing called 'free will' that God gave to each of us which separates us from the animals. Human beings do not just function based on instinct. Each of us has free will in our decision-making until the day we die.

One last, very important lesson from Proverbs 22:6 that I believe is often overlooked is the importance of the developmental stages of childhood as the time that training is most critical to the rest of a person's life. The Hebrew word used in Proverbs 22:6 for child "focuses on the child's young formative years."[107] If we do not actively train our children in the way that we believe is the right way to live when they are young, the chances of them choosing that path in adulthood are greatly decreased. Research conducted by the Barna Group in 2004 reveals that 43% of professing Christians in America made their commitment to Christ before the age of 13, and 64% made a commitment to Christ before they turned 18.[108] On the other side of the issue of the importance of early experiences in a child's life, studies show that "individuals who begin drinking alcohol before the age of 15 are about 7 times more likely than those who start after age 21 to develop alcohol problems."[109]

There are numerous studies demonstrating unequivocally that the first five years of life are extremely critical to the well-being and healthy functioning of the individual for the rest of his or her life. Dr. Clyde Hertzman, an early learning scientist at the University of British Columbia, and his team of 200 researchers have led the way in determining how early childhood experiences influence brain structures, sensory pathways and functions. According to Hertzman:

> "the biological 'code' of success in life is built by all the sounds, sights, touches, thoughts and emotional interactions that children experience in their first few years. The team's stunning bottom-line conclusion is this: If children don't get what they need during the crucial developmental 'windows' before the age of five, they likely will never bounce back."[110]

Often, emotional and psychological damage that is done to a child in the first five years of life is practically impossible to overcome without intense intervention and a miracle from God. Conversely, proper training in the first five years of life can impart emotional, psychological and spiritual strength to an individual that gives them the ability to stand against the *Cultural Tsunami* of the world that desires to take them down the broad road to destruction.

I have observed a couple at my home church who took this early training very seriously with their young son. They lovingly drilled as much Scripture as possible into his little brain in the first five years of his life. He could recite entire chapters of the Bible effortlessly. This young boy enjoyed reciting Scripture and took any and every opportunity to show off his ability to recite long passages to the amazement of others. For the rest of that little boy's life, the truth in those Scriptures will come to mind at critical times of decision. That is more powerful than a million lectures from his parents!

In biblical times, young Jewish students began studying Scripture at the age of 5 and most had memorized the Talmud (the entire Old Testament) by the time they were 14.[111] Are children in the twenty-first century less intelligent or capable than these Jewish children? I don't think there is any evidence to support that conclusion. We need to take the spiritual training of our children very seriously. Many of us treat our children as though we don't believe we can expect too much out of them academically. Most parents completely entrust the education of their children to the secular public school system and the spiritual training of their children to once-a-week Sunday School classes. In today's culture, our children need to be armed for battle with "the sword of the Spirit, which is the word of God."[112]

****

So many of the Scriptures I memorized in my life were as a child participating in Bible verse 'sword drills' in Sunday night Training Union (the equivalent of evening Sunday School.) If you grew up in a Southern Baptist church you know what this is. A sword drill started with the leader saying in a commanding voice: "attention." At this command, we stood straight and tall with our Bibles at our sides. Then the leader commanded: "draw swords." In response, we held our closed Bibles out in front of us. The leader then announced a verse, i.e. John 3:16, then shouted "charge!" Whoever found the verse first stepped forward and read it aloud. At the time, I thought it was fun to be able to find verses faster than anyone else. The leaders made a point of having us find critical, foundational Scriptures over and over and eventually the verses were memorized. Through these sword drills, I became adept at navigating my way through the Bible.

The AWANA program that is in so many churches across the country today also does an amazing job of helping parents instill Scriptures into the hearts and minds of children while the kids are having fun earning badges and trophies and competing in all kinds of games. With all the resources and support available, there's no excuse for Christian parents in the United States to drop the ball on this component of spiritual training in the first five to ten years of their children's lives. Think about it. If you knew that a literal tsunami was coming when your child hit the age of 12 and there was no way to leave the geographical area, would you just throw up your hands and hope for the best? I doubt it. I think you would do absolutely everything in your power in those 12 years to train your child in very specific survival skills so his chances of surviving the tsunami were as high as you could possibly make them. Many children today are not surviving the *Cultural Tsunami* because they did not receive the diligent, intentional spiritual, emotional and psychological training they needed to stand up against it.

Training is an active, goal-directed process that requires consistency. It does not happen haphazardly. When we just take it as it comes and wing it as parents, the result is going to be hit or miss, regardless of whether our hearts are in the right place or not. I would challenge you as a parent that if you are parenting in a haphazard, inconsistent manner, your heart is most likely not in the right place. However, for you parents who are just waking up to an adolescent or teenager in your home who is being overwhelmed by the *Cultural Tsunami* and you realize that you've missed opportunities to prepare them in the first few years of their life, take heart! Believe me, I know exactly how you feel! Whatever you do, don't give up! Yes, you have a very difficult few years ahead of you but there is so much you can do to face this challenge. It's never too late to change course. Keep reading and remember that God is a God of redemption and second chances. "Jesus looked at them and said, "With man this is impossible, but with God all things are possible."[113]

CHAPTER 10

SPARE THE ROD,
SPOIL THE CHILD?

Another oft-quoted saying attributed to the Bible that many Christian parents use as justification for hitting their children, and many non-Christians use to label Christian parents as abusers, is really not found in the Bible at all. The well-known adage that is often attributed to the Bible, "spare the rod, spoil the child," was originally published in 1662 in a poem by Samuel Butler called "Hudibras."[114] It is based on Proverbs 13:24, which states: "He who spares the rod hates his son, but he who loves him is careful to discipline him."[115] There is a similar verse in Proverbs 23:13-14 that says: "Do not withhold discipline from a child; if you punish him with the rod, he will not die. Punish him with the rod and save his soul from death."[116] Wow! God really means business when he tells us to take responsibility for the training and discipline of our children. He says that it's a matter of life and death!

So, it sounds pretty simple – go out and get a really big rod and begin beating your children tomorrow, right? Isn't that what it says? That type of misinterpretation is what happens when we pluck a verse or two out of the Bible and attempt to apply it out of context. For that all-important context, we can look at the description of how a Christian, who is controlled by the Holy Spirit, behaves, as described by the Apostle Paul:

"But the fruit of the Spirit is love, joy, peace, patience, kindness, goodness, faithfulness, gentleness and self-control."[117] The Apostle Paul goes on to say that "Those who belong to Christ Jesus have crucified the sinful nature with its passions and desires."[118] If we are controlled by the Holy Spirit, will that affect how we parent, even in the most challenging moments? Of course! Especially in the most challenging moments! When we, as Christian parents, have been pushed beyond our human limits both emotionally and physically, we must exhibit the self-control that comes from walking closely with God. Sometimes having self-control will mean we walk away at the moment, calm down, say a prayer, and deal with the situation tomorrow.

Our sinful nature thinks selfishly in that moment of confrontation with our teenager. We remember all that we have done for our children and think about how ungrateful they are. We desire to knock some sense into them or at least make them feel really guilty for what they are doing to us! But, once again, it's not about us! Keep your focus on the bigger picture. This is a spiritual battle for the hearts, minds, and very lives of our children. We have been placed in our children's lives as their guiding shepherds and we can learn a lot from examining the way a shepherd deals with challenging, wayward sheep.

When we read a verse in the Bible that refers to the importance of using the rod of correction on our children, doesn't it make sense that we would find out how a rod is typically used in the context in which it is being presented? All through the Psalms and Proverbs, the rod and stafvf are described in the context of a shepherd and his sheep. The Lord is described as our Shepherd in the 23rd Psalm. The psalmist says to God: "Thy rod and thy staff, they comfort me."[119] How can something we're being beaten with be a comfort? The psalmist also says: "we are His people and the sheep of His pasture."[120] The New Testament calls Jesus the Good Shepherd[121], the Great Shepherd[122], and the Chief Shepherd.[123] I believe this metaphor, which is presented throughout Scripture, is a picture of how the parent/child relationship is to look, as God also calls Himself our Father and describes us as His children.[124]

The book *A Shepherd Looks at Psalm 23*[125] by Phillip Keller gives a beautiful description of the shepherd/sheep relationship. Keller provides a very clear picture of how a shepherd guides his sheep and how he uses his rod and staff, which explains how the rod and staff were a comfort to David (who wrote the 23rd Psalm). The shepherd understands the life and death nature of his responsibility for his sheep and is alert at all times. He knows that without his constant guidance and correction, they will wander off and most surely die. He has educated himself regarding the many predators that are lying in wait for the sheep that are under his care, and he is prepared to fight them off. The shepherd is willing to break the leg of a sheep that repeatedly wanders into danger. Whatever it takes to protect his sheep and keep them on the right path, he will do – out of love and concern for the well-being of his sheep, and ultimately to keep them alive.

Keller describes the rod of the African herdsmen he observed as a child:

"The rod was, in fact, an extension of the owner's own right arm. It stood as a symbol of his strength, his power, his authority in any serious situation. The rod was what he relied on to safeguard both himself and his flock in danger. And it was, furthermore, the instrument he used to discipline and correct any wayward sheep that insisted on wandering away."[126]

Keller reminds us of the significance of the rod that God gave to Moses when He sent him to deliver the Israelites from Egyptian bondage:

"it was his rod that was to demonstrate the power vested in him. It was always through Moses' rod that miracles were made manifest not only to convince Pharaoh of Moses' divine commission, but also to reassure the people of Israel."[127]

155

Keller makes the point that the strength and authority represented by the rod provides comfort to the sheep in knowing that they are well-protected and that someone strong and confident is there to guide them. He also describes the disciplinary use of the rod in the hand of the shepherd:

"There is a second dimension in which the rod is used by the shepherd for the welfare of his sheep – namely that of discipline. If anything, the [rod] is used for this purpose perhaps more than any other.. If the shepherd saw a sheep wandering away on its own, or approaching poisonous weeds, or getting too close to danger of one sort or another, the [rod] would go whistling through the air to send the wayward animal scurrying back to the bunch."[128]

The protection aspect of the rod in the hand of the shepherd is equally important, as there are many predators in the life of a sheep. Keller describes the protective use of the rod:

"It is used both as a defense and a deterrent against anything that would attack. The skilled shepherd uses his rod to drive off predators like coyotes, wolves, cougars or stray dogs. Often it is used to beat the brush discouraging snakes and other creatures from disturbing the flock."[129]

Keller describes an experience he had in Kenya as he was photographing elephants, accompanied by a young shepherd. The shepherd boy saved their lives when he skillfully used his rod, in a split second, to kill a cobra that was ready to strike. So I ask you this – does your teenager have any coyotes, wolves, cougars, stray dogs or even cobras in his/her life? What are you doing to drive them off?

I have a few questions that I want you to consider in the context of that loving shepherd/sheep relationship that Keller himself witnessed firsthand and describes for us in his book. Do you believe that the shepherd Keller describes takes his rod and beats the sheep as a release for his own frustration and anger because "they just won't listen?" After a particularly long, trying day, do you believe that the shepherd smacks the sheep when they make noise and get on his nerves? Do you believe that when the shepherd feels overwhelmed by all of his responsibilities, he blames the sheep and randomly whacks them with his rod? If the shepherd was insecure and inconsistent in his leadership, do you think the sheep would respond respectfully to his direction? If the shepherd was distracted by his own personal issues, how long do you think it would be before he lost a few of his sheep? Do you believe that the shepherd takes into account whether it is a young sheep, an adult sheep, or a sheep that repeatedly wanders when he reacts to foolish or dangerous behaviors? The shepherd only breaks the leg of a sheep that repeatedly wanders into danger, refusing to learn from previous warnings, as a last resort to save its life. There are many ways that we can symbolically 'break the leg' of a wayward teenager that we will talk about later.

****

Now, in the interest of full disclosure, I confess that I spanked my children when they were little. I intended to spank in the Dr. Dobson way, which is not in anger but in a very controlled way, only in cases of willful disobedience, and rarely, if ever, after the age of 10.[130] However, my son Chris could tell you that I spanked him totally out of my own frustration more than once. I did not cross the line into what would be classified as abuse. It typically consisted of slapping his arm or his clothed butt with an open hand. I remember one time using a belt on his butt, through denim jeans, but that time was in a very controlled manner. I didn't flail away at my kids with a belt or any other object, just with my open hand, and never across the face. However, back in the day, I was known to throw things across a room – kind of an adult version of a temper tantrum! And unfortunately for my children, I was a screamer for the first 10 years or so of my role as a parent. I

157

confessed that sin and abruptly stopped that indulgent, immature behavior one day after throwing a shoe and realizing how
foolish I looked to my wide-eyed children!

I remember one time spanking Michelle and Heather with a
belt across their little 5-year-old clothed bottoms. The spanking
consisted of a couple of controlled whacks. It was more for
effect, although I'm sure they will tell you that it was traumatic
to see Mommy getting out a belt, which had never happened
to them before. The offense that I believed warranted a belt
was a game of "Blues Clues" (remember the PBS children's
show?) in the unfinished basement of our next door neighbor
with the neighbor's younger daughter. They took markers and
drew clues all over the walls and furniture in the neighbor's
basement. When the neighbor called to tell me what she had
found in her basement, the girls received a stern talk about
what they had done, a couple whacks on the butt with a belt,
then we went over with a bucket and cleaner, they apologized
to the neighbor and we cleaned it up as much as possible.
They were old enough to know that you don't write on walls
or furniture, especially at the neighbor's house! I really don't
remember spanking them any other time, except maybe
a slap on the hand or butt to get their attention. The same
goes for Rebecca, who I don't really remember spanking. She
has memories of carrying on so dramatically when she got in
trouble that I softened and didn't spank her. I also think that I
was so preoccupied with Chris's defiance that Rebecca probably got away with a lot! She was so sweet that it was hard
to get angry about anything she did. I'm sure you've noticed
that there's no mention in this chapter of my husband Paul
spanking the children. He never spanked the girls and rarely
spanked Chris. As a result of his own childhood experiences,
he had a strong aversion to administering stern punishment
and his long hours spent at the office and traveling during the
early years left most of the disciplinary decisions and imple-
mentation to me. Anyway, if plain old indiscriminate spanking
was the magical answer to defiance, Chris would have turned

out to be the model adult at the age of 18, and this book would be all about the benefits of spanking!

I had an interesting experience with Michelle and Heather. They were adorable little identical twins and received a lot of attention any time we went out. People doted on them at church and strangers made comments when we were out grocery shopping or at the mall. I'm sure other mothers of identical twins have experienced exactly what I'm talking about. The girls learned from an early age to use that cuteness to their advantage. They outwardly appeared to give us no trouble at all. They rarely had tantrums and did not talk back. They were very loving and sensitive little girls. However, one day I woke up when they were about 5 years old and abruptly realized that they rarely complied with my instructions. When I told them to pick up their toys, I would come back a few minutes later and be met with the same mess on the floor and two sweet faces saying "We're sorry mommy. We forgot." This pattern repeated itself all day every day. I realized they were sweet-talking their way out of obedience on a regular basis. This type of disobedience is no less sinful and wrong than more outward demonstrations of disobedience. From that day forward, my expectations and response changed and the girls' behavior began to change.

The purpose of this personal disclosure is to demonstrate the dilemma that I believe most parents face. Think about all the dynamics in that description of my personal experience with discipline and corporal punishment. It is almost impossible to not be influenced by our own emotions as we discipline our children, either going easier on the "sweeter" child or harsher with the "difficult" child. As good as my intentions were, once I allowed myself to consider spanking as an option, I was unable to avoid using corporal punishment in an uncontrolled, angry, frustrated manner with my most strong-willed, defiant child. I'm sure there were periods of time when Chris received a spanking daily with many of them being more about my own frustration than about what he had done. However, when it came to my seemingly compliant daughters, that option never seemed to be a desirable response. Imagine the message Chris must have gotten as I angrily whacked away at his butt day after day, then rarely if ever reacted in that manner when the girls disobeyed in a more subtle way.

Spankings, as with yelling and screaming, quickly become ineffective when used frequently. Kids have an innate ability to become accustomed and desensitized to our behavioral patterns as parents, no matter how shrill or loud our screaming may be. However, when a parent who is usually calm and even tempered suddenly raises their voice or gives the child a whack on the bottom, that's powerful stuff. It gets the kid's attention and affects them deeply. They take notice and determine not to repeat whatever caused the parent to respond so strongly. Sometimes kids will push the even-tempered parent to see how far they can go before the parent lays down the law. Once they find out that there is a point where the parent will take a more forceful stand, the child typically backs off.

The spanking administered to Michelle and Heather when they drew all over the neighbor's walls and furniture seemed to have the desired result. I wanted to make a point about that behavior that would stick in their minds and prevent them from ever crossing that line again. A lecture just didn't seem to cut it. My response was more about training them than about releasing my own frustration or anger. It worked because, by that point in my parenting, I had gained a little more maturity and self-control and it was not the typical response they got when they disobeyed on a smaller scale. Therefore, they never forgot that lesson. I have come to believe that spanking should only be used as an absolute last resort in extreme situations, and should only be administered in a controlled manner.

The verses in the Bible that we take to be a reference to corporal punishment are, in fact, a stern caution to parents to realize what is at stake when we are raising our children and that we must be willing to take even extreme measures when necessary, like the shepherd who breaks the leg of the perpetually wayward sheep, to save our children's very souls. It may mean removing our children from public school. It may mean moving to another part of town. It may mean giving up a second income temporarily so one parent can be home. It may mean taking away the cell phone, the computer, the television, and our child's freedom (which to a teenager is the equivalent of symbolically breaking their legs). We must be willing to take these types of extreme measures. Whatever sacrifice and non-abusive action is required on our part to bring a child into an attitude of submission to authority which also promotes that child's ability to submit to God and achieve his or her purpose in this life, we must be willing and ready to do, no matter how much of an inconvenience or hardship it is on us. After all, it's not about us!

CHAPTER 11

THE BRICK WALL OF AUTHORITY

If you ever took an introductory Psychology class in school, you probably read about the experiment that was done with a group of elementary aged children. They were placed in a large field, with no visible boundaries, and told they could play anywhere they desired. The children stayed together in a pretty tight group. The same children were placed in a fenced-in yard to play. Instead of staying clumped together, they spread out to the edges of the boundary and ran freely using the entire space they were given.[131] The obvious point of this experiment is that children feel freer, safer, and more confident when they are given clearly-defined limits. When children aren't sure where the limits are, they often experience fear and anxiety. They will often respond by pushing perceived or threatened limits farther and farther to see if any true limit exists that will actually stop them. They want to know that there is a limit they cannot get past. It's very much like the sheep with their shepherd in the earlier chapter. Sheep will follow their shepherd because he is a confident leader who has set clear, consistent limits and will exert his authority to protect them and keep them on the right path.

****

As I described in the chapter entitled "Train up a Child," my husband and I were pretty weak in the area of authority when our first two children were small. It wasn't that we didn't love our children and want to be the best parents we could be. We were living in the moment not realizing how important setting firm, immovable limits in the early years was to the future of our children. I believe that most parents who will take the time to read this book really love their children and desperately want to do the right thing.

Parents are often insecure in their role. I believe that many of us fear that our children will withdraw their love from us if we are too hard on them or make them unhappy. Many parents today experienced at least one divorce of their own parents when they were growing up. Children of divorce have felt the deep agony of rejection and abandonment when one or the other parent leaves (I discuss the long-term ramifications in the chapter on divorce). As a result, we often go into parenting with the mistaken notion that our children will always make us feel loved and secure. We create a family of our own that we believe will never leave us or reject us.

Ask yourself how you feel when your child, no matter what age they are, says hateful things to you or withdraws from you. I believe that our children are capable of churning up deep emotions within us that have been buried since we were children ourselves. These are feelings that we never wanted to experience again. If we don't deal with our own personal insecurities and fears, they have the potential to affect our parenting in a destructive way. We will be responding to our children out of our own personal fear of rejection.

Our children smell our weaknesses and know exactly where the buttons are that they can push to get their way, especially strong-willed children. Remember, children are born with a self-centered core. At about 12-18 months of age, the battle of the wills begins. If you recognize that you have insecurities and fears of your own that interfere with your ability to parent confidently, please deal with the root of those inse-curities. There are many good books that will lead you through Scripture to address your specific issues (I highly recommend any and all books written by Joyce Meyer). Once again, *The Purpose-Driven Life*[132] by Rick Warren is a powerful book that uses Scripture to speak truth regarding our significance and purpose in life. Spend time talking to God about your deepest heart issues. Ask Him for healing and ask Him to reveal to you those things you need to deal with to experience wholeness. Face those hurtful issues from the past and allow God to flood you with his healing, love and peace. If you have access to a good Christian counselor, they can walk you through the process of healing.

We often look to the feedback and reactions of others for information that reassures us that we are good parents. We place way too much emphasis on what others think of us and our children. Let's look at the information we get from the feedback of others. Most of us are very receptive to compli-ments regarding our children. We dress them a certain way, sometimes pierce their ears at a young age, and style their hair when they are just toddlers (or even babies), then we soak up the attention and comments about how absolutely adorable they look. I really had fun with this when Michelle and Heather were babies. I got so much attention every time I took them out in public because they were the cutest little twins you every saw! (Oops, I'm falling into that trap again!) Seriously, we soak in that positive response as though it has something to do with our parenting. All it says is that I was willing and able to bathe my child, comb her hair, buy cute clothes and dress her up. Of course this demonstrates that I am not neglecting the basic hygiene and physical care of my children, but it says absolutely nothing about the effectiveness of my parenting.

The other danger in judging the effectiveness of our par-enting against the reactions and feedback of others is that so many other parents are falling into the same traps we are. They are not qualified to judge whether we are parenting well. And, we know our own children better than anyone else (except God). Other people watching us interact with our children have no idea what our goals are, what our child's temperament is and why we are dealing with them in a certain way. For this reason, I am resistant to making judgments about the parenting choices others make in public places.

I recently was in line at our local Kmart behind a woman with three small children. The youngest little girl looked about 2 years old. She had thrown herself on the floor right in front of me and laid there crying while the mother paid for her purchases. I talked to the little girl as she laid there. She would look up at me and stop crying briefly then start back up again. When the mother was finished paying she scooped up the little girl, put her in her shopping cart and left. As soon as she was out of earshot, the clerk at the register and the woman behind me immediately launched into harsh criticism of this mother. I said to both of them that we know nothing about what kind of mother she is and that this may have just been a moment of frustration. I had a few moments of frustration when my four children were small.

****

Another trap we often fall into is judging our parenting based on the happiness of our child. That is definitely not the barometer we should measure our parenting against. What does the happiness of my child tell me about my parenting? Not much. We have to realize that our children are immature, self-centered little people. They don't know what's good for them. It is very easy to make a child happy. All we have to do is give them what they want in the moment. Have you seen any of those morbidly obese young children on television talk shows? The mother of one of these children said she has to give him food constantly because he is sad if he's not eating. She is willing to risk his very life because she can't bear to see him unhappy. Now we might not be shoveling food into our children's mouths, but we often do this very same thing in other ways.

I believe that many of us need to change our entire perspective on parenting. We must realize that being a good parent means that we will feel very badly at times, our child will not be happy with us a great deal of the time, and that the rewards for good parenting are not immediate. The ability to tolerate bad feelings and patiently await positive results requires a level of maturity on the part of the parent. Effective parenting requires tremendous personal sacrifice and self-denial.

****

The Brick Wall of Authority is a visual image of the attitude that I believe is desperately missing and is needed in many of today's parents. The absence of this Brick Wall of Authority is, I believe, responsible for the lack of respect for authority that is one of the overarching themes of this book. The Brick Wall of Authority is what we must become at those times when our children directly challenge our authority. Imagine a brick wall that you can't climb over, you can't dig under, you can't get around, and you can't break through. It doesn't waiver or move and it doesn't talk, yell, beg, or cry. It doesn't attempt to explain its existence. It's just there. You can spend hours or even days trying to break through it or climb over it, but you're just wasting your time and energy. You can stand there and bang your head against it as long as you want until you finally realize that all you are accomplishing is giving yourself a monstrous headache! Finally, you come to your senses and give in to the immovable strength and authority of the brick wall. You might be angry with the wall for not moving, crumbling, or engaging in an argument with you, but your anger doesn't change anything. The brick wall is still the brick wall! It's the kind of authority that the Shepherd demonstrates with his sheep and that God demonstrates with us. God's authority doesn't change just because we don't like it and the Ten Commandments haven't changed since God gave them to Moses.

So, how often have you been that brick wall with your children? I would presume to guess that most of you have tried to be the brick wall at times but ended up wavering or crumbling before ultimately turning into a wobbly bowl of gelatin! Maybe you consider yourself to be pretty strong in the area of authority, but I challenge you to ask yourself if you are a parent who takes a strong posture then allows a small crack to open up in the wall that allows your child to slide through to the other side, ultimately getting what he or she wanted all along. The lesson our children take from that is that when we decide to take a stand, all they need to do is beg, whine, yell, stomp, argue, plead or threaten enough to outlast us and turn us into gelatin, or at the very least chisel a crack into the wall. They get their way and all is well with the world because they are reminded that they ultimately hold the power.

This Brick Wall of Authority is not about making a lot of noise and proclamations about being the boss. It's about our actions, not our words. The fewer words we use at times of direct challenge, the better. Once we've crumbled or allowed a crack for our child to slide through, we often try to make ourselves feel better by making some idle threat in the child's direction, like "if you don't come home by midnight, you've had it!" There's no way that child is going to be home by midnight and what exactly does that threat mean anyway? Who knows? It doesn't matter because the child in this scenario is in control, not the parent, and they know it!

****

How often do we find ourselves verbally running around in circles with our children (or feeling like they are verbally running circles around us) in an effort, as well-meaning parents, to help them understand why it's important that they brush their teeth (or whatever else we need them to do)? I actually had the frustrated mother of a 7-year-old describe to me her efforts to get her son to understand the high cost of dental care and the negative social implications he will face if he doesn't brush his teeth every night. She was frustrated that he didn't understand and accept the importance of brushing his teeth. When you think about it, the attempt to get our children to agree with and fully understand our requirements in order to gain their compliance is an easy way out for parents. It places the blame squarely on the child and their lack of under-standing. It's no longer about our refusal to exert our authority or their willful disobedience. Of course, this approach didn't motivate the 7-year-old to brush his teeth and it never occurred to the mother that it was okay to exert her authority over her child with confidence and without a full-blown explanation. This dance can happen between parents and the youngest of children – as early as the child is able to utter the words "no" or "why."

The belief that a child is owed an explanation for every-thing their parent expects of them seems to have emerged from our society's increasingly child-centered approach to the behavioral challenges of children. Just the other day, I heard yet another well-meaning parenting expert on televi-sion explaining why he believes that parents should never say no to their children. The reasoning is that the child will not learn anything from a simple no. Therefore, if the parent is not allowing their child to have something, the parent must take the time to explain to the child why they can't have what they want. The way this type of parenting usually plays out is that by the time the parent finishes attempting to explain, the child has argued and begged his way into getting what he wanted and the parent is left exhausted and frustrated.

If you have a verbally skilled child, you know that they often love the argument and have the energy to keep going until we collapse and give in. Verbally sparring with our children lowers us to their level. It sends the message that whoever has the best argument or can argue the longest wins. It also teaches children that there's a potential reward in arguing with adults. It has nothing to do with respect and authority.

It has been my experience that the moment in which a parent is saying no to their child is usually not a teachable moment beyond the basic establishment of authority. The child is not going to hear and process the explanation in that moment. All the child knows in that moment is that he wants something and someone is standing in his way of getting it. Sometimes it's not so much about the issue at hand but more about the child's determination to not submit to authority. I believe that the most desirable end result of a moment of challenge to a parent's authority is a scenario where the parent remains calm and their authority remains intact. Later, when we are having a peaceful, one-on-one moment with our child is the time to have a conversation about why they are not allowed to do or have certain things whether they understand or agree with our decision or not.

****

I have become increasingly convinced that the accepted notion of a child's behavior being his or her own 'choice' has done damage to our families and schools, and potentially to our society at large. This approach assumes that the child will respond well to a reasonable, rational approach that offers the child options. We have begun teaching children to stop, then think, then act with the idea being that when they stop and think, they are to consider the consequences of their "act" before acting. Then, when they act, they will have consequences either good or bad to face as a result. The reality often is that the well-intended consequence is either watered down or never actually occurs. Even when an appropriate consequence is implemented, I'm concerned about the lesson being learned by the child.

This concept has some positive elements that sound good on the surface. The child is learning personal responsibility for his or her behaviors, the child is encouraged to not blame others for their own actions, and the child is learning that there are consequences to his or her actions. What can possibly be wrong with this approach?

Let's dissect the 'choice' behavioral approach[133] that has become so prevalent in our culture. While it seems to have all the benefits mentioned above, how could this approach possibly be damaging to children, families, schools and the culture at large? Let's look at this from the child's perspective. In the most basic scenario the child reaches for a cookie that they have been told they are not allowed to have before dinner. The child-centered mother, who wants more than anything to be the best possible mother, says to the child something like "Mommy told you no cookie before dinner. You need to make a good choice."

I have frequently seen mothers talk to their 3-year-olds this way. The child looks at Mom and looks at the cookie. The child takes the cookie and sticks it in her mouth. The typical mother is going to scold the child, maybe use emotional punishment by telling the child that Mommy is disappointed in her, then threaten that she can't watch "Dora the Explorer" that day. Mom might even use the popular time-out consequence. What has the child learned through this process? The child has learned that she holds complete and total decision-making power and authority in her life. If she chooses to disobey the authority figures in her life, it's an equally acceptable decision as obedience would have been as long as she stops to consider that there may or may not be a negative consequence that follows her choice.

This idea of children being offered choices that they alone hold the right to decide between is devoid of a foundation that acknowledges the existence of absolute right and wrong and an ultimate authority over them. Right and wrong are within the child and totally subjective. In our culture, we bend over backwards to avoid exerting our basic innate authority as parents. It seems that we have become convinced that the authority God has given us as parents is a bad thing that we must rein in and subdue. Therefore, the child becomes the authority over himself. There is no Brick Wall of Authority that the child cannot get around. If Mom labels one choice as the "bad" or "wrong" choice, that is the mother's subjective opinion. It is inferred in this approach that it is up to the child to determine which option is the best personal choice for them at the moment. They only need to consider the possible consequences in making their decision. It's all about the cookie and not about an authority figure requiring obedience.

Sensitive children will put more weight on the possibility of disappointing their mother or father as they make their decision and Christian parents will throw in the possibility of disappointing God to further influence their child toward the preferred choice. However, many children can tolerate Mom's or God's possible disappointment if they want that cookie badly enough. Some children learn at a very young age the pattern of disobedience followed by a quick "I'm sorry" to get what they want then receive immediate restoration into Mom's and God's good graces. No true repentance and no consequence to follow.

The choice approach leaves the choice-making to the discretion of the child's own reasoning and ability to control his or her own impulses. Let's take this to the next level. The child is in elementary school and another child has left some money in plain sight on his or her desk. The child is left to his own reasoning and impulses in that brief moment when deciding whether to take the money that doesn't belong to him. There is often no sense of a Brick Wall of Authority at home that requires that the child obey the rule against stealing that has been set by the school, by the parents and by God. There is just a possible negative consequence to consider, if he gets caught.

Even if the child knows in their moment of decision that Mom would consider taking the money to be a "bad" choice, the child has been given the sense that he is at the center of his universe and is his own authority. It is left up to him to judge the rightness or wrongness of his choice. He only has to consider that there may be a consequence to pay, if he gets caught. The other side of that coin is that no one is looking so he will probably not get caught and the money will be his.

If we take this child-centered approach into the teenage years – and by then it is deeply ingrained into the child's core belief about who he is in relation to the world – we have teenagers 'choosing' to fearlessly stand up to teachers and an educational system where the most serious consequence is typically a few days in detention. The choice approach creates teenagers who refuse to respect their teachers unless their teachers "earn" that respect. Granting respect is also a 'choice' they have the right to make.

I often tell teens that their parents and teachers deserve their respect simply because of the positions of authority they hold. This is a very important distinction. Teenagers do not understand the concept of respect for authority that is based solely on the position of the authority figure. The teenager sees respect for authority as something that he or she has the power to choose to grant if, and only if, they decide the teacher or other adult deserves it. When I have asked teens exactly what a teacher would need to do to earn their respect, I have never once gotten a clear answer. I have a feeling there is not a clear answer to that question. It is totally subjective and up to the teenager to determine at any given time. Teenagers speak more about liking or not liking teachers which is typically based upon the personality of the teacher, how much fun the teacher's class is, how accommodating the teacher is to the student and how good the teacher makes the student feel. Once again, granting or not granting respect originates in the self-centered emotions of the child. We all had our favorite teachers when we were in school; however, teachers should not be required to play up to their students to curry their favor and hopefully be granted basic respect in the classroom. A foundation of respect needs to exist the first day a student walks into a classroom before that student even knows whether they like the teacher or not. Unfortunately, the choice approach has taught today's children that they hold all decision-making power and that nothing is absolute.

It should not surprise us that in this climate there seem to be more and more teachers engaging in sexual activity with underage students. The separation created by the clear distinction and understanding that the position of teacher carries great authority over the position of student immediately sets a boundary between the teacher and student on day one. This separation or boundary has been watered down almost to the point of nonexistence in today's schools. We have elevated students to a level of authoritative equality with teachers.

Our society today acts outraged when teachers are caught having sex with underage students; however, the media coverage and consequences imposed by courts are beginning to demonstrate the ambivalence that is truly at the core of our culture. When I was growing up, there were teachers that we students considered to be 'hot'; however, if there was even a suggestion that a student was having a relationship with a teacher outside of class it was shocking and considered by most everyone to be an outrageous offense. Such behavior required the breach of a major boundary that was understood and accepted. That boundary rarely exists anymore in the minds of many teachers and students.

****

It is the rare teenager today who has been required to respect one or both of his or her parents just because they are the parent. Most teenagers have ways that they get around the authority of their parents, which completely undermines any respect they might otherwise have for their parents. Would you automatically respect someone you could outsmart and weasel your way around? Would you respect parents who daily, from the time you were a toddler, reminded you that you are the decision maker regarding what you will or won't do? Would you respect parents who seemed hesitant and insecure about owning their own authority and basically relinquished their authority to you, a mere child? Would you respect parents who made big, blustery pronouncements then rarely if ever followed through?

Parents often merely seem to be the presenters of options and consequences to their children. Many parents and day-care centers send the message to children every day that the child himself is the ultimate authority who decides which choices are right based simply upon the rewards or consequences waiting for him following his decisions. And so often the consequences or rewards are not even consistent. Giving children this much power results in extremely frustrated parents and teachers who can't understand why children are out of control.

Unfortunately, in many cases the very first Brick Wall of Authority a child ever runs into in his or her life is law enforcement. Even then, quite often the parents and those around the teenager or young adult come to their rescue and attempt to help them find a way out of the mess that they have in most cases created. The most passion I often witness from parents is when they are defending their children against consequences being administered by another authority figure in their child's life.

****

When I was growing up in the 60's and 70's, our parents were beginning to be challenged by a more child-centered view emerging in our society. In the 50's, it was seen as good parenting to stand in authority over children and it was expected that children would accept the authority of adults without question, both at home and at school. If kids were disruptive in school, they often faced the dreaded 'belt' or 'switch' when they got home. I am not in any way suggesting we go back to threatening our children with or using physical punishment. Perhaps at that time we went too far in stifling children's feelings and questions which possibly created a generation of adults who resented authority figures. Quite possibly this approach in the extreme actually taught children very little about making decisions for themselves and when the authority figure was removed, the child was at a loss when it came to decision-making. Maybe mothers of that generation said that awful phrase "because I'm your mother and I said so" too frequently. However, it seems that the pendulum has swung too far in the other direction when even occasionally uttering that phrase is a reason to beat ourselves up and feel like we have failed as parents.

It seems to me that the pendulum needs to swing to a more balanced approach between the two extremes. The problem I am seeing with parents today, and I'm talking about involved, caring, committed parents, is that they seem to be looking for permission to exert their God-given authority over their children. In my therapeutic practice, I have frequently seen a look of great relief and a little surprise on the faces of parents when I encourage them that it's okay to "lay down the law" in their home and "require" that their children do the very things they least want to do, without a lengthy, detailed explanation.

I think it's a pretty sad commentary on our society when we need commercials on television leading us to government websites whose sole purpose is to teach parents how to talk to their children! If my conversations with parents are any indication, doing the dishes seems to be one of the biggest battlefields in homes today. There is also the fear of damaging the child's self-esteem that usually goes hand-in-hand with today's child-centered approach to parenting. Coddling is damaging to a child's self-esteem. Appropriately requiring respect and obedience builds self-esteem.

I am all in favor of imparting our beliefs and values to our children by allowing them to question our decisions in a respectful manner at an appropriate time. However, this questioning of our decisions is not acceptable in the heat of a challenge to our authority. There are teachable moments, when we are not in the heat of conflict. However, I believe that kids need to know that there will not always be a nice, neat explanation for why they have to do certain things or behave in particular ways. Also, I believe that we do not owe our children an explanation every time they ask for one. Often, the reason we are requiring a certain behavior from our children is beyond their understanding at their current stage of development. There need to be times when the only reason a child has to do something is because an authority figure required it of him. Or in everyday terms, "because I'm the Mom and I said so."

No one I know of in the history of the world was required to obey in a more outrageous situation than Noah.[134] God told him to build a huge boat, on dry ground, because water was going to fall from the sky (which it had never done before this time). For Noah to follow through on this seemingly ridiculous task, he had to completely trust God and have the utmost respect for His authority. Have we trained our children to trust and respect us to the degree that they will obey us even if they don't understand or agree with the reasons we are requiring a certain behavior?

****

I have laughed with friends who remember, as I do, growing up with a healthy fear of our parents. There were many times I chose not to do something simply because my parents would have "killed" me if they found out. Of course, I did not literally fear for my life and my parents didn't beat me. The phrase 'my parents would have killed me' refers to that Brick Wall of Authority that requires and expects obedience to authority and a set of absolute rules. There was no doubt that my parents were the authority in our home, not the children. For example, I didn't believe that I had a choice in deciding whether to take something that was not mine.

Unfortunately today many children are not given the gift of a belief in a just God who gave us the Ten Commandments without asking what we thought about them first and Who fully expects us to obey them. God says "Thou shalt not steal."[135] We know, as Christians, that we can trust that God is a good God and that everything He says or does is for our good and His glory. However, if we believe that He is the Ultimate Authority over us, we are willing to obey the Ten Commandments 'just because He said so.' Sometimes that has to be enough of a reason not to do something.

What do I propose as a solution to the situation I have described? The only thing I know for sure is that parents need to fearlessly reclaim their authority in the home without apology. Own your authority with confidence! I'm not suggesting that you turn into a bully ordering everyone around. I'm saying that you need to stand firm and confident and require your child to submit to your authority. It's much more about an attitude and belief in your God-given authority in your home. Yes, your child will challenge you and will try to divide and conquer you and your spouse. You and your spouse must stand together as a united team supporting each other's authority.

What is it about these little people that brings us, the adults, to our knees? Do not be intimidated by your children. Don't let them rattle you. Ask God for wisdom and guidance every day, then exhibit calmness and confidence as you take responsibility for your family. I encourage parents that it's okay to require behavior from your child just because "you're the parent and you said so." There's a time and place for this Brick Wall of Authority to come into play and for the child to be required to submit to it without explanation.

I tell all parents who come into my office that even if they don't go to church themselves, their children need to be taught that there is an authority greater than the parents. At the very least, every parent needs to send their child to the church of the parent's choosing where their children will be taught a foundational belief in a good and just God Who is the authority over all. If you work on Sundays, send your children to church with a relative, neighbor or friend. As Christians, we know that the best and most effective scenario is for the whole family to go to church every Sunday and for the parents to acknowledge the authority of God in their own lives. However, those of us in the church can stand in the gap for kids whose parents drop them at the door for Sunday School, Youth Group or Vacation Bible School.

As a parent, you have been given permission (and the responsibility) by God to say to your child "because I'm the parent and I said so" without apology and without beating yourself up. You hold the position of authority in your home. You need to claim it and your child needs to know it!

CHAPTER 12

SETTING GOALS AND MAKING IT HAPPEN

Getting your priorities and parenting goals figured out in a logical, non-emotional manner is an exercise that I don't think many typical parents work through. Most of us just figure we'll learn on the job and take it as it comes.

Probably one of the most significant driving forces in the way we parent is the desire to either be just like our own parents or the complete opposite of our own parents (or some mix of the two). I agree that it's good to learn from our own experiences growing up, but this can be a trap. We can get so stuck in our determination to be the opposite of our own parents that we go to the other extreme. Both extremes, permissiveness and authoritarianism, can be equally ineffective. If we are so focused on being just like our own parents, we will lose sight of the moment we are living in that may require a completely different approach.

We need to develop our own set of priorities and goals based on the qualities we desire to instill in our children. So get out a piece of paper and a pen and write down, in order of importance, the qualities you would like your child to possess as an adult. If you have an involved spouse, have them make a list as well and compare the two. Then come up with a joint list that best describes the qualities you are attempting to instill in your children. These are your intentional goals. This is a very important first step to clarify what you need to do as parents before you find yourself in the heat of an emotional battle.

The qualities we believe our children need to develop to be successful in this world must be required of them as they are growing up. It's just like exercising our muscles. We have to develop strength over time through repetitively exercising the very qualities we are looking to develop – especially the difficult qualities. In addition, we absolutely need to be straight-forward and real with our kids in every situation. Manipulation often has a more negative effect than doing nothing at all as a parent. The good old "guilt trip" might work in the moment with the more compliant child but I can promise you that your kids will come to resent you if you use the guilt trip as a tool to control them. Kids hate this approach and parents fall back on it way too often. It will come back to bite you later on in the parent/child relationship.

****

A young mother recently asked me for ideas on how to begin instilling the quality of delayed gratification in her young daughter. I encouraged her to not shy away from opportunities to have her daughter practice saying no to her flesh. Typically, we parents avoid the dreaded toy aisles in our local Wal Mart like the plague or resentfully give in to our child's persistence when they are throwing a fit in public. How are our children supposed to learn to accept disappointment in an appropriate, self-controlled manner if we don't give them a chance to practice and develop this emotional skill? At the same time, we need to clearly express our expectations for their behavior when they are disappointed. Consistently avoiding any and all situations that might create a negative emotional response in your child is not good parenting – it's actually a selfish approach that avoids the need to exert your authority as a parent. This strategy might make your life easier in the moment, but it actually prolongs the need to continue this avoidance strategy, which will really complicate your life.

You will inevitably end up in situations that are a challenge for your child. If you have not trained your child to accept no, you will have a major meltdown on your hands when you are forced to say no or someone else says no in a situation you cannot avoid. How is that fair to your child? They are eventually going to hit a wall where the answer is no. Every child needs to learn to accept no, the earlier in life the better. You have done your child a major disservice if you do not require your child to accept no for an answer from a very young age.

Occasionally walking through the toy aisles at Wal Mart and admiring the toys with the understanding that nothing is going to be purchased that day, then expecting your child to accept the disappointment of not taking home a toy, is an opportunity for a growth experience. Even if your child does not respond in the way you want them to, they will learn that 'no means no' and over time they will learn to accept no. In between these lessons, there should be times when they are allowed to pick out a toy within a budget that you have set ahead of time. Telling a child that they have a specific budget that they have to stay within is also an opportunity for a tremendous lesson in accepting limits as a natural part of life.

Saying no to our flesh almost always creates a negative emotional response within us. If we never learn to deal with bad feelings as a part of life, we will forever be looking for a quick escape or an immediate outlet for those feelings. With young children, the outlet for bad feelings is usually a temper tantrum directed at the parent. The old adage "misery loves company" is so true! When we feel badly, even when we are very young, we want to make the person closest to us suffer right along with us. The temper tantrum is a very effective outlet that indulges the child's negative feelings and also serves the purpose of drawing the parent right into the middle of those bad feelings.

Regardless of what causes negative feelings inside a child (sleepiness, hunger, thirst, disappointment), the child often feels that they cannot tolerate being alone in those feelings. And what do we, the parents, usually do? We indulge their desire to have us emotionally join them and jump right into this emotional trap, often adding our own negative emotions to the mix. The result is two (or more) miserable, upset, loud people engaging in a temper tantrum together. The child learns that this temper tantrum thing does the trick when they are feeling badly! We need to act like adults and remain calm, not giving in to the tantrum. If your child is crying or throwing a fit, ask yourself why. If they are sleepy, hungry, thirsty or just overstimulated, your response needs to be comforting and their needs should be met as soon as possible. However, if they are throwing a temper tantrum just because they did not get their way, a calm, firm approach with an appropriate consequence is in order.

Sometimes avoidance of potentially upsetting situations is necessary, but avoidance needs to be the exception, not the rule. Remember, you must parent boldly with specific goals in mind. Be diligent to notice when your child exhibits an appropriate response to disappointment and reward them. I strongly encourage parents to use relational rewards such as a special one-on-one activity with you. You know your children and what they really enjoy doing. If they have a favorite book, read it with them. If they have a favorite game, play it with them and really engage. This will very deliberately teach them that accepting no when their flesh wants a material possession will lead to a much better relational reward. They will learn to value good feelings that come from relationship over material pleasures.

Remember the chapter on drugs where we discussed how pain pursues pleasure? We need to teach our children from a very young age that emotional pleasure comes from healthy relationship rather than material possessions or other destructive things the world offers. Sadly, parents sometimes use material rewards as a substitute for relational rewards, which require an investment of their personal time and energy. As a result, kids learn that good feelings come from things, not from relationships. If you are saying to yourself "I don't have time for all this training and relational reward stuff," answer this question: Do you have time for all the impromptu temper tantrums or acts of disobedience that are in your future? It's one of those situations where you either pay now, or pay dearly later.

The scenario described above may not fit perfectly with your situation. Think about the areas of conflict you are experiencing with your young child then fashion a plan that fits within your child's triggers and personality type. Don't expect that your child will respond perfectly the first time you put your plan into action. It will most likely be very messy the first few times you implement this training strategy. However, don't give up. Make it a process that you and your child repeat on a somewhat regular basis.

Remind your child how much fun you had when you played the board game or whatever else you did when they responded appropriately. If they continue to throw tantrums every time they are faced with disappointment, don't give up. It just means that your child has a strong-willed temperament. Engage in the fun reward activity with them at other times so they know how much fun the reward will be when they respond appropriately. Then when they're sitting in time out, remind them that you would much rather be playing a game with them. Keep at it and don't give up! Remain calm and don't give in to your frustration.

Every child is different and if your child does not respond right away, it's all the more reason to not give up. If your strong-willed child learns that if he keeps going you will eventually cave in, he will attempt to outlast you every time you require obedience. Make sure you outlast him! (A perfect example of this is "Jimmy's Story" in chapter 13.)

****

Special rewards for good behavior need to be creative. Sometimes kids themselves come up with the best ideas.

The Cultural Tsunami

Something we did in our house as the kids were growing up was to have "appreciation nights". We did them randomly and often the person was surprised. We might announce at dinner that it was Heather appreciation night. Then we would go around the table and each person would describe a quality that they especially liked or appreciated about Heather. It sounds so simple and a little hokey, but it's amazing how good that person feels and the laughter and good feelings that are generated as each person says something positive about the person of the day. Teenagers enjoy this, even if they won't admit it. It also forces siblings to say something nice about each other, which doesn't always come naturally. It's great to do an appreciation night when siblings aren't particularly getting along. It forces them to think of something positive to say about each other, even if they have to get very creative. If you respond with laughter at their feeble attempt to compliment their sibling, warm feelings are created in the moment, however brief it may be. If I wanted to make an appreciation night extra special, I would make the honored person's favorite meal that night. For Rebecca, the special meal always involved pasta and never potatoes! Imagine how you could use this reward with a three or four year old who resisted throwing a fit when they really, really wanted something they couldn't have at Wal Mart. They would be king or queen of the dinner hour! Their amazingly wonderful behavior would be the star of the evening and the story would be recounted to everyone present. You may even want to call Grandma to sing the praises of their amazing grandchild, in earshot of the child. This is what true character building in a young child looks like. Just imagine how this deliberate training will manifest itself in the life of your child when they enter adolescence.

****

So, whatever stage of parenting you find yourself in, ask yourself this question: what specific behaviors do I want my child to exhibit when he or she reaches adulthood? Or, to put

186

it another way, what are the most important qualities I want my child to possess when he or she reaches adulthood? It is never too early to ask yourself this question. You can also ask yourself, "What particular behaviors do I need to extinguish in my child?"

When you decide which skills and character traits you would like to develop in your child, the ideal time to begin this deliberate training is before your child reaches adolescence. When your child is 18-24 months old, they will begin to exert their own will by saying "no" to you, running away from you or hitting you. That is your first opportunity to begin this important work as the parent. Just yesterday, my daughter and I were in the waiting room of our pediatrician's office. We observed a young mother attempting to get her approximately 2-year-old child to leave the office and go to the car. She coerced, begged and pleaded with him as he completely ignored her and continued playing with toys. Finally, she pretended to be leaving without him and said something like "you'll just have to live at the doctor's office." How effective do you think this approach was? I know first-hand that it may work with compliant children, but this never works with strong-willed kids. I know because I did exactly what she did in different forms when my older two children were toddlers.

A more effective approach is to walk over to the child, squat down to their level and say their name, and then tell them that it's time to leave and go home. If they resist, firmly take their hand and walk them to the car. Once again, you must respond with confidence and an expectation that your child will ultimately obey you. If they don't respond to a firm approach and go limp or fight against you, pick them up and take them to the car. With as few words as possible, say to them that they will not behave this way and will leave when you tell them to. If they submit at that point, walk them to the car. If you are in a position where you have a baby in a carrier or other children with you, do whatever you have to do to get them to the car in a decisive manner. Don't waste a second with coercing, begging, bargaining, pleading, or yelling. React decisively and quickly. The longer it takes you to exert your authority, the more the child becomes invested in their decision to take a stand against you. The child needs a clear message in that moment. Drive home in silence. The child knows what he or she did. When you get home, implement whatever consequence works with your child (sitting in a chair facing the corner with no interaction, being put in bed without any toys, no favorite TV show that day, etc.) Once the consequence is fulfilled, with as few words as possible, tell your child that he/she will not ignore and disobey you like that in the future. No excuses. End of discussion.

A firm, clear statement in a serious tone of voice stating what the child WILL do in the future is what is required - NOT "Mommy really wants you to listen and be good" in a childlike, whiny, pleading voice. What exactly does that mean anyway? A child needs to hear a clear, specific statement of what they will do because you are requiring it of them. One day I was with a mother and her four-year-old son in a doctor's office. The little boy kept running around the room, annoying other patients. The mother repeatedly, in a timid voice, said to her child "be good" and "stop being bad." Her little boy completely ignored her and enjoyed the reactions he was getting from everyone in the room. Finally, I asked the mother what she wanted her son to do. She said "I'd like him to sit in the chair." I instructed her to pick him up and put him in the chair while telling him that he must stay in the chair. Every time he got out of the chair, I instructed her to firmly pick him up and put him back in the chair, reminding him that he must sit in the chair. After 3-4 times of this, he finally stayed in the chair and was given a book to look at. Ideally, it's best to prepare your child for the environment you are taking them into and your expectations for their behavior in that environment. If you find yourself unprepared, decide in the moment what behavior is acceptable for your child, then give them specific instructions with the expectation that they will obey. You must respond to disobedience quickly in a firm, confident, controlled manner with as few words as possible.

It is our job to train our children and prepare them to live in this dangerous world. The vast majority of the parents I have spoken with or counseled describe having had this type of power struggle with their child. The situation usually revolves around the parent trying to get their child to do something the child does not want to do. Sometimes it's just about control and has nothing to do with the issue at hand. In most cases, the parent engages in a back-and-forth dialogue with the child trying desperately to explain their position. I've got news for you – in the heat of the conflict, your child doesn't care to hear your explanation. In the moment, they are entrenched in their position and all that matters is getting their way.

A mother I know described the frustration of telling her adolescent that she was being required to accompany her for a weekend visit with the extended family. The daughter did not want to go because she would much rather spend the weekend having a sleepover at her friend's house. The daughter had an emotional explosion accusing her mother of not understanding or caring about her social life and how important it is for her to spend this time with her friend. She went on to tell her mother how desperately her friend needed her because of all kinds of drama in her life, blah, blah, blah. How did the mother respond? She engaged verbally and emo-tionally in this dramatic moment by having a contest with her daughter over whose weekend plans were more important. The mother argued back that the daughter didn't understand how important this weekend was to her and how much she misses the relatives and how her daughter should miss them and want to visit them too, blah, blah, blah. Such unnecessary silliness doesn't accomplish anything and actually undermines the authority of the parent. It also models for the child that this type of immature emotional response is an appropriate way to get what you want.

If you have decided that it is important for your adolescent to accompany you on a weekend trip to visit extended family, then they are going. No argument. Of course, when things calm down and your child understands that they are going, you can and should listen to their reasons for not wanting to go and you can state your reasons why you are requiring them to go. You can always reverse your decision if after consideration you determine that your child has valid reasons not to go. But if your child throws a temper tantrum, their reasons will not be heard. The minute the tantrum begins, discussion is over. They will only be heard and responded to if they present their position in a calm, respectful manner. So while the child is throwing the tantrum they must be ignored completely. At a calm, teachable moment the subject may be revisited with a reasonable discussion about why you believed it to be important that she accompany you on the trip. If your child calms down and approaches you in an appropriate manner, it is appropriate to hear and validate her reasons for not wanting to go. However, it is not necessary for your child to agree with your decision. Ultimately, the decision is yours to make and theirs to respect and obey.

Somewhere along the line between the 1950's and now, we got the idea that we owe our children an explanation when we require something of them. As the experts say, we have become a child-centered society. It's not enough just to require something because we're the authority figure. Parents are often visibly surprised when I tell them that they don't need to explain every decision to their child and that it's okay to require something of their child even if there isn't a significant, meaningful reason for doing it (as long as it isn't going to harm them in some way and causing them unhappiness is not harming them!).

How on earth do we expect our children to say no to sex, drugs, drinking and a multitude of other negative temptations when they've never been expected to accept no in other areas that they didn't understand? We wonder why our kids don't seem to listen to authority or take it seriously. They haven't been required to! We have pleaded, begged, threatened, and explained ourselves silly in a polite, often manipulative manner in an effort to convince our children of what they should do.

It is my personal opinion that this approach has created a disrespectful, confused generation.

****

I find that moms are particularly vulnerable to their own emotions when they are faced with a defiant teenager. Our teenage children know what our weaknesses are and an emotional mother is particularly easy to overpower. To help the mothers I have worked with in my practice, I developed a persona that I call "Robot Mom." I instruct mothers with defiant teenagers to become Robot Mom in those moments of direct confrontation. Robot Mom displays absolutely no emotions. She is the personification of the Brick Wall of Authority. She is matter-of-fact and uses few words. She states her expectation or her decision about what is going to happen and cannot be flustered, no matter what the teenager says or does. This is basic "Operant Conditioning," as developed by B. F. Skinner when he was at Harvard University in the 1920s and 1930s:

> "To put it very simply, behavior that is followed by pleasant consequences tends to be repeated and thus learned. Behavior that is followed by unpleasant consequences tends not to be repeated and thus not learned."[136]

Of course there is more to this theory, but when we remove emotions from our response, exert our authority in a confident manner and implement a positive or negative consequence, defiant teenagers take notice.

One single mother with a particularly defiant teenage son had tried every possible emotionally-based response to make their mornings more tolerable. This young man would refuse to get out of bed until the absolute last minute. Once he was up, he dragged his feet, refused to take his medicine, and made her late to work almost every morning as she waited in the car for him. She found herself begging, pleading, yelling and lecturing all morning every morning and was an emotional wreck by the time she got to work. I instructed her to tell him in a very matter-of-fact way that he was responsible for himself in the morning. He was told that if he wasn't in the car by 7:15 she was leaving without him. Of course he became angry in response to her perceived threat and his nasty comments increased as he rose to meet the challenge. He was determined to break down her resolve so that her threat would never materialize. If he didn't take his meds, she told him, that was his problem and he would have to deal with the repercussions at school when his hyper behavior made it hard for him to sit in class. Then came the tough part - she had to follow through and ignore him all morning long as she got herself ready for work.

Sure enough, when she got in the car at 7:15 he wasn't ready. He had to challenge her threat to prove that she wouldn't follow through and things could go back to how they were before, with him in control. She backed out of the driveway and left for work. All the way to work her cell phone was ringing as he was trying to call her. He couldn't believe she actually did it. It took all the emotional strength she could muster to ignore her phone. She checked with the school later to see if he got there. Sure enough he had ridden the bus to school. Of course, he was extremely angry with her when she got home that evening and he began berating her for being a terrible mother. After all, how could she leave her child at home when she knew he had to get to school? She became Robot Mom again and very briefly stated, in an unemotional manner, that this was the way their mornings would go from now on. She told him that if he wanted a ride to school, he had to be in the car by 7:15. The next morning, he was in the car early waiting for her. He wasn't happy, but he realized he had no choice but to comply if he wanted a ride to school. (Now, in this case we're talking about a 17-year-old boy in a suburban area. You wouldn't leave an elementary school-aged child at home alone. You would apply a different, age-appropriate behavioral technique to get the same result.)

The point is, you pick a battleground and take a stand. Then you make absolutely sure you follow through with your promised response. The trick is that this must be done in a non-emotional manner with as few words as possible. Your child may challenge your response over and over but ultimately they will learn that they must do what you require or an undesirable result will occur. Another lesson your child will learn is that only through cooperative behavior will they get what they need – a ride to school. Often, extremely defiant adolescents' and teens' defiant behaviors are being rewarded when we yell, beg, plead, and freak out at their defiance. They feel empowered and completely in control, which is often a reward for them. We must not reward negative behaviors. Remove the reward by remaining calm and outwardly unaffected. Your child must not succeed in breaking you down. Defiant children know where their parent's buttons are and they will push every one of them to get the desired response. When a defiant teenager says "I hate you!" or "I wish I lived with Dad!" in most cases they don't mean it. What they are really saying is "I hate that you are requiring me to submit to you!" This behavioral approach really does work in most situations of direct defiance. The benefit that results from calmly responding with confident action, few words and no emotion usually spills over into other areas of defiance as the child now wonders if you might decide to stand up to them in those areas as well.

In extreme cases where a single mother has an especially defiant teenager, I instruct them to call the police if their teenager takes off or becomes threatening or aggressive. Younger siblings should never be put at risk. A trusted man in the church who has a relationship with the teen and can provide authoritative backup for the mother can be a real asset. The defiant teenager needs to know that a higher authority will be called in if they cross the line into behavior that endangers their family or themselves. In some situations, when a mother is alone in the home and the teenager's behavior is out of control, the teenager will need to be sent to live with his/her father or some other relative. In the most extreme cases if no relative is available to take them in, the teenager may need to go to a residential facility.

B. F. Skinner believed that this non-emotional, operant conditioning approach was the answer to all parenting and societal issues. Skinner came to the extreme conclusion that:

"virtually all behavior is controlled by the contingencies of reinforcement that occur constantly in the environment. The notion of behavioral freedom is thus an illusion."[137]

As Christians, we know that God created human beings with free will and much more complexity than Skinner's approach acknowledges. I believe that a behavioral approach can be effective in particular situations, especially with direct defiance from an adolescent or teen. However, the ultimate goal of parenting is to point our children to Jesus Christ and to develop in them a spirit of submission to authority that will allow them to submit their lives to the will of God.

****

In direct contrast to Robot Mom, our culture describes a good parent as someone who is friends with their teenager, hangs out with them, buys them a cell phone and all the other high tech gadgets, understands that their child will probably have sex and party but just expects them to keep it within acceptable limits, doesn't come down too hard on their child for any offense, and heaven forbid, never embarrasses their child! The highest compliment that parents aspire to is to be called "cool" by their child and his/her friends. Basically, what this means is that you don't get in the way of whatever your teenager and his/her friends want to do, and sometimes even actively assist them in their never-ending quest for fun, popularity and excitement. And what's even more amazing is that other parents are envious of the "cool" parents that are liked by the teenagers. In our insecurity we wonder "why don't the kids like ME?"

Everyone knew who the coolest parents were at my daughters' public high school. They regularly provided the party house for the football team and cheerleaders and other kids privileged enough to be invited, buying kegs of beer and pizza practically every weekend. Finally, one of their parties was busted and they were arrested along with two other adults who participated. Several football players and cheerleaders got kicked off their squads. Needless to say, our football team had a losing season that year. I recently read in the paper that these parents were given an opportunity at a plea deal that required them to apologize to the entire student body at a school assembly. If they accepted the deal, they would not be required to face a trial and possible jail time. The parents refused the deal and are going to court. Now, I don't have first-hand information regarding the details, but it seems to me that they are still on a quest to maintain their coolness in front of their kids and their kids' friends. How embarrassing would that be for them and their kids if they stood in front of the entire student body at the school their kids still attend and admitted their guilt and apologized. It looks to me like they would rather risk jail time than risk losing their cool status in the eyes of their kids and their kids' friends. Wow!

So I encourage you to do some soul searching and ask yourself honestly, "what am I motivated by when I make decisions as a parent?" Are we just like the party parents, only on a smaller scale? Maybe we wouldn't buy beer for our kids, but do we back down and give in to our teenagers in hopes that they will appreciate us more? Do we find ourselves giving in to avoid a blowup with our teenager? Do we say yes to things because we're concerned about what other parents will think of us if we say no to our kids? Is our parenting more about us than about what's best for our teenagers?

****

So let's talk about the teenage outburst. It's very similar to the toddler temper tantrum so the same type of Brick Wall of

Authority response applies to teenagers as well. Strong-willed kids are really good at making their outbursts very effective. When you have a situation where you believe that you need to say no to your child or teenager, do you recoil out of fear of their reaction? Been there, done that! Strong-willed teenagers can outlast us and intimidate us in ways we never imagined. When they want something, they will push whatever buttons it takes to get it. They typically don't mean a word of what they are saying in that moment. Words mean nothing at the point of confrontation. They are merely tools in the hands of a master manipulator attempting to get a desired result, which in this case is a parent who has crumbled and given in to their demands.

Look at confrontation as an opportunity to train your children. Don't hesitate to say no to things that your gut tells you are not good. That gut feeling is often the Holy Spirit speaking. Typically, the stronger your teenager reacts, the more your decision is confirmed as the right one! If you start to weaken and fear that you are being overprotective, talk about it with someone you trust who has the same moral values as you. It's so important to have fellow parents who are on the same page as a support system. However, in most cases in today's culture, parents are going overboard in the direction of permissiveness, overindulgence and mixed messages. If you are deliberately training your children, you will rarely make decisions that match up with what all the other parents are doing. Get used to standing alone!

Our mindset as parents today is very wimpy. Heaven forbid we are the one parent who doesn't let our child have something or attend a particular event. We often cave to peer pressure as easily as our children do. We don't want to be the parent that no one likes and we want our kids to be popular and included. We also long for that smile and hug we get from our child when we let them go somewhere or have some-thing, even against our own better judgment. Maybe we need to go through boot camp ourselves to learn how to tolerate negative feedback from our children, from their friends and from other parents.

Remember the shepherd? His sheep were comforted and happy because they knew he was confident and in control, with their best interest as his top priority. He drew the lines where he believed they needed to be with very clear goals in mind then enforced those limits with boldness and confidence. If we have our own happiness as our top priority, we will be distracted by and make decisions based on our own emotions, not the best interest of our children. Unfortunately, our child's best interest and our own happiness often clash. That's why we need to be clear in our own minds that our top priority is the well-being and training of our child.

If we have to cancel plans because we need to stay home to monitor a teenager, oh well! Even if the plans are a weeklong cruise we've been looking forward to. You can take nonstop cruises in a few years when your children are out of the house. If you can't take your child with you, don't ever leave him/her home alone overnight. That is the riskiest thing any parent with a teenager can do. Teenagers will promise his or her parents the world to be left home alone for a few days. Even typically responsible kids will do things they wouldn't normally do when given that level of freedom. And when peers find out there's a house where parents aren't home for a few days, they will be drawn to it like a magnet. That typically responsible child will be faced with peer pressure like never before. If you have to go out of town and you can't take your teenager with you, leave him/her in the care of the strictest person you know. Putting our children first is not a matter of coddling them and making sure they are happy. Often, teenagers are happier in the moment if we are distracted chasing our own happiness. They like being their own boss and think they are mature enough to be out partying and making their own decisions. Even if they seem to be, they are not!

****

There seems to be some confusion going on in the minds of today's parents. Perhaps we think that 'happiness' and 'feeling good about ourselves' are the same thing. They are not even close to being the same thing. Happiness is a momentary, surface feeling that is often attached to a set of circumstances. Feeling good about ourselves is a much deeper, more profound experience that is not dependent on circumstances. It is based in our belief about who we are as an individual, no matter what is going on around us. When we feel insecure about our own value as a person, we seek out ways to feel better about ourselves. We are not giving our teenagers the opportunities they need to feel really good about who they are as unique individuals! This is instilled in a person through the experiences of facing difficult challenges in life and successfully coming through them. To instill a positive sense of self in our teenagers, we must allow them to experience unhappiness. As parents, we feel good when our children are happy, but in reality we should be feeling good when our children are successfully dealing with unhappiness.

Girls today are so easily taken in by the sweet talk of boys, which indicates just how desperate they are to feel special. The blame for their neediness most often lies squarely on the shoulders of their fathers. I strongly recommend that every father of a daughter reads the book *Strong Fathers Strong Daughters*.[138] If Dad has totally abandoned his daughter, she needs a strong, positive father figure in her life. Secular studies have recently shown that a father is the most influential person when it comes to shaping what a girl thinks about herself. If a father listens intently to what his daughter has to say from a young age, without talking down to her, she learns that her thoughts are valued and significant. If a father takes his daughter with him when he goes on errands, he shows her by his actions that she is good company and fun to be with. If a father asks his daughter for her opinion on something, she learns that her opinion is valuable and important. If a father challenges his daughter to exceed her own expectations, she learns to believe in herself because her father believes in her.

If a father is physically affectionate in an appropriate way with his daughter and tells her that he loves her, she learns that she is deserving of love and affection. There is absolutely no excuse for a father to drop the ball in this important relationship, if he is allowed to spend time with his daughter, which he should absolutely fight for. Dads, your daughter will relate to boys and will conduct her life based on what she has learned about herself through your eyes. If you leave her mother and start a new family, she sees that as abandonment of her. She will believe that she wasn't important enough or valuable enough for you to want to stay with her and that she is easily replaced.

Some of the saddest situations I see are when parents split up. Now I know there are cases where it cannot be avoided and abuse should never be tolerated. However, often parents who just aren't getting along or aren't "happy" believe the lie that things will be better for everyone if they split up and that they will both equally spend time with their children after the divorce. Be the grown up and make the right decision for your children, even if it's not what you want to do at the time. Your children only have a brief 18 years during which a foundation for the rest of their life is being built. You owe it to them to give them a stable family unit in which to grow and develop. Remind yourself every day that you are giving your children a gift that is more important than any other and that this is not your time, it is theirs. Seek out counseling, a pastor, and/or friends who can provide support, a listening ear and the love you need to help you persevere. Commit your life to Jesus Christ and to your children.

What most often happens following a well-meaning divorce is that pretty soon one or the other parent begins dating or remarries. New relationships become important or a whole new family is formed and that parent's attention is demanded by someone else. Where does that leave the 'old' children? They feel completely cast aside as they see their father or mother focused on a new relationship, parenting someone else's children, or new kids of their own with a new husband/

wife. On top of it all, they are told to be nice and not cause problems in either home so they don't get in the way of their parents' new lives. I saw a very sad situation develop in a family where a mother with a young daughter divorced her husband. She met someone and re-married, then had more children. The first husband also re-married and had more children. This woman's second marriage fell apart as well. Her children from this marriage stayed with their father as she pursued a career. The oldest child didn't know where she belonged. This young woman didn't feel she could stay with the step-father because it wasn't her 'real' father but she couldn't go back to her biological father because he had a new family. Her mother was rarely home because she was pursuing a career. So this young woman was left pretty much alone, not feeling like she belonged anywhere.

Parents, it's time to grow up and put your children's well-being ahead of your own happiness. Provide the very best environment possible when they are growing up. Your children deserve to have their very own parents all to themselves until they are grown. If you must, divorce and pursue your own happiness once they are grown and out of the house.

CHAPTER 13

YOU HAVEN'T MET A KID AS BAD AS MINE!

This chapter is a very special one. It's a personal gift from me to parents who are at the end of their rope, barely hanging on by their fingernails. I've been in your shoes. My heart goes out to parents who are at that place, believing that there is no situation worse than theirs and no adolescent or teenager more defiant than theirs. I'm talking about loving, concerned parents who believe they have tried everything to no avail, but are still willing to give it one more shot. With God's guidance, the majority of clients who come into my office in this state of mind receive hope and help to turn things around with their child.

I believe the best way to offer hope to you is to present a couple of real-life examples of radical transformations I have personally witnessed. Chances are you will see components of your situation in one of these examples. Of course, names have been changed to protect confidentiality.

JIMMY'S STORY

Jimmy's family was referred to me when I worked as an in-home therapist. Jimmy was six years old at the time. He lived with his mother Beth, his father Steve, his ten-year-old sister Lily and his grandma. They all resided in grandma's modest home. It didn't take long to see that Jimmy was the person in charge and that the three adults in the home were intimidated by him.

Beth and Steve were good people who loved their children. They had experienced a professional setback that required them to move in with Grandma until they could get back on their feet. Their confidence had been shaken by this setback and they were embarrassed by their children's defiant, disrespectful behavior, especially in Grandma's house in front of Grandma. Grandma was frustrated but tried to stay out of it. She spent a lot of time cooking or running errands.

After spending a few evenings with the family, observing and interacting with each of them, a clear pattern emerged. Little Jimmy liked to do whatever he wanted, whenever he wanted, without interference from adults (what child doesn't?). He went outside to play whenever he wanted, came back inside when he was good and ready, ate in front of the television whenever he wanted, refused to go to bed until he decided it was time, brushed his teeth if he felt like it, came to the dinner table if he liked what was being served, if he didn't like what was being served he got snacks out of the cupboard, and on and on. If any of the three adults in the home dared to require something different than what Jimmy wanted, an explosion of monumental proportions occurred. The length, volume and intensity of the explosion were dependent upon how long it took for the adults to back down. Jimmy went as far as destroying his own bedroom, turning his mattress over and breaking things when his parents required him stay in his room. Of course, his mother came along and put it all back together for him before he went to bed that night.

Now when I say explosion, I mean explosion of the nuclear variety. This kid didn't care who was hurt as he kicked, punched and threw things. One evening, with fear and trembling, I observed as the parents, at my direction, intentionally triggered a meltdown. All they had to do was turn off the television and tell Jimmy that he was going to bed, whether he liked it or not. The meltdown began with defiant yelling in their faces and repeated attempts to turn the television back on. At my prompting, Steve picked up Jimmy and carried him upstairs, with Beth trailing behind with the most fearful expression I have ever seen on a mother's face. Jimmy began screaming "You're choking me! I can't breathe!" That was all it took for Beth to lose it. She began crying and demanding that Steve put Jimmy down before Jimmy got hurt. And that was the end of it. Jimmy ran into the loving arms of his mother, sobbing as though he had been victimized in some way, all the while glaring at Steve. Beth sat on the sofa cuddling and comforting Jimmy. I sat in my chair trying not to throw up!

I had all the information I needed to see what was going on. As we processed this pattern and everyone's role in it, Beth acknowledged that she couldn't stomach seeing Steve become physically forceful with the kids, even if all he was doing was picking up Jimmy and carrying him upstairs. Beth also acknowledged that she couldn't tolerate the condemning looks and comments from Grandma when one of the children threw a fit. Little Jimmy knew this and used it to his advantage. Both parents acknowledged that something had to change and that they needed to regain their authority as parents.

The plan we devised looked like this: A chair was set up facing the corner in the front room. We called it the "think about it" chair. The idea was that the parents were determined to outlast Jimmy, however long it took. Grandma was informed of the plan and was assured that Jimmy would not be hurt in any way, no matter how loudly he screamed. Jimmy was told about the "think about it" chair and was informed that any time he disobeyed his parents, he would receive one warning. If he still refused to comply or ignored them, he would be placed in the "think about it" chair. He didn't seem too concerned.

The evening came when the plan was put into motion for the first time. Jimmy was told it was time to turn off the TV and go to bed. The usual defiance ensued. Jimmy was warned once as he pushed past his father and turned the TV back on. When he ignored the warning, Steve picked him up and placed him in the chair. The three of us stood around the three sides of the chair and barricaded him in. No one was to touch or grab him in any way and Beth was instructed to say loving, comforting things to Jimmy reminding him over and over that when he calmed down she would take him up to bed and read him a story.

Two long hours of screaming, pushing, and hitting (by Jimmy) ensued, with short breaks while Jimmy regrouped and caught his breath, only to start up again. We adults stood firm and only used our hands and arms to defend against Jimmy's flailing. One of the biggest eye-openers for Beth was when Jimmy started screaming "You're choking me! I can't breathe!" when no one was even touching him. Finally, very suddenly, Jimmy collapsed into the chair and fell fast asleep. Beth picked him up and lovingly carried him upstairs and tucked him in bed. It was a turning point for the entire family. From that point forward, on most occasions of defiance, all it took was for Steve and Beth to warn Jimmy that he was going to be placed in the "think about it" chair for him to comply with their directives. They had to follow through with the threat a few more times, but it no longer took two hours for Jimmy to calm down and comply. It's important to note that no one hit, slapped or yelled at Jimmy. These parents had merely out-lasted him. Another interesting side effect of the process was that Jimmy's sister Lily had observed everything and became much more respectful as well.

BRANDON'S STORY

So, you may be dealing with a teenager who is out of control. Picking them up and barricading them in a chair is not an option. However, the same basic principles apply. You need to figure out where your power lies and boldly determine to outlast them as you exert your authority. Let me share with you the true story of a teenage boy I'll call Brandon.

Brandon was a great kid! He had been homeschooled through 8th grade. His mother and father had a decent marriage and he had two little brothers, Jason (10) and Jeremy (5). The family went to church faithfully and Brandon had friends in youth group. He wasn't really close to anyone his own age but he had always seemed content staying to himself until 8th grade.

Brandon began bringing up a desire to go to public school. The town they lived in had a well-respected school system and a newly-renovated middle/high school campus. It was within walking distance of their house. The kids in the neighborhood were a close-knit group and Brandon saw them walking to and from school every day. Since he didn't have school in common with them, he had been unable to break into the group. He would see them going into each other's houses to hang out. He felt more and more left out of life.

Brandon's parents discussed the possibility of Brandon going to public school in 9th grade. They had never had any trouble with him. He was obedient most of the time and only gave them a little backtalk here and there. He pretty much left his little brothers alone. Brandon's mom was already wondering how things would go with homeschooling when Brandon got into the more difficult high school curriculum. Maybe this was the answer. They made the decision to enroll him in public school for 9th grade.

Brandon's 9th grade year was uneventful. He became involved in the Jr. ROTC program at school and was quickly rising to the top in the program. Brandon's mom felt good about the academic instruction he was getting, as well. She had done a good job with homeschooling up to that point and Brandon was right on track, if not ahead, in all of his classes. Then Brandon started hanging out with some of the neighborhood kids.

None of the neighborhood kids ever seemed to want to come to Brandon's house, but Brandon was always asking to hang out at their homes. Brandon's attitude abruptly began to change – especially toward his family. When Brandon's parents said no, Brandon's response was loud and forceful. He became argumentative with his parents and critical of his family as a whole. He began closing himself up in his bedroom more and more. At the end of 9th grade, he announced that he wanted to drop out of Jr. ROTC.

Monitoring Brandon that summer became extremely difficult. He would leave the house without saying where he was going and would get in his mother's face when she tried to stop him. Finally, summer was over and the new school year began. Brandon's parents didn't see any way they could return to homeschooling Brandon because his negativity would have a profound effect on his little brothers' schooling. His mother didn't think she could handle having him home all day, especially after the summer they just experienced.

Brandon was still hanging out with his group of friends from the neighborhood and had a new girlfriend, as well. He seemed to have a secret life and was becoming sneaky when he was home. He guarded his book bag and his cell phone and avoided looking his parents in the eyes. Instead of just being annoyed by his little brothers, he acted as though he hated them. His grades were slipping in every class. Brandon's parents decided that they needed to know what was going on. One day when he went to his girlfriend's house they searched his book bag.

They sat in stunned silence as they held in their hands papers that seemed to list prices and amounts of what looked to be marijuana. On the list were first names, ounces and amounts owed and paid. A search of Brandon's bedroom followed. They found a bag of something that looked like pot and drug paraphernalia. They determined to call the school the next day and make an appointment with the Principal's office.

When Brandon got home they said nothing and allowed him to close himself up in his room. They had confiscated the list and the drugs and paraphernalia. Brandon went straight to bed and didn't notice. Brandon's Dad took off work the next day and they made plans for the younger brothers to be picked up by their aunt in the morning. Brandon took off for school, as usual, not knowing anything was different. The parents made the appointment and took what they had found to the meeting.

Brandon was called out of class to the Principal's office. His life would never be the same again.

Brandon's parents were united and fearless. As upset as they were emotionally, they were determined to do whatever it would take to give their son a chance to get back on track, even if it meant harsh consequences for their son. The police were called and the list was confiscated. Brandon was given probation because it was "only marijuana" and the amounts were so small. He was required to fill in last names on the list. Brandon's parents took away all of his electronics and his freedom. He had recently gotten a job at the local grocery store and his driver's license. He was told that his parents would only be driving him to and from work and that he was not allowed to drive anywhere himself. When they discovered that he was borrowing cell phones at work and calling his friends on breaks, they talked to the manager of the store who began monitoring Brandon more closely.

Brandon made their home environment as difficult and unpleasant as possible. He would get in his parents' faces and yell at them. He would argue them around in circles when they had any conversation with him. It was his only recourse. When they first brought him into my office, we spent the first two sessions in circular conversations. Brandon would answer a question with a question. The only communication strategy that worked was for me to state an assumption I had about him then see if he corrected it or argued with me. The third session, he did one of these round and round debates with his mother about something totally nonsensical in the waiting room in front of me. When we got back into my office, I called him out on it. I told him that I saw what he was doing and that he had been doing the same thing to me. I told him that it was a very clever strategy. He then made the first honest statement I had heard from him. He said "It's the only way I can tip the balance of power." This was one smart kid and he knew exactly what he was doing.

Two things became very clear over the next few weeks. Brandon could not extricate himself from the situation he was in with his group of friends. And Brandon was a bundle of emotional contradictions. He had bonded with these friends through pot smoking. Participating in drug use with others creates a strong emotional bond. His parents had two very clear options. Their first option was to just continue like they were over the next year of Brandon's high school career and deal with Brandon's issues the best they could until he graduated. The second option was to intervene in a way that physically separated Brandon from his peer group. In counseling sessions, we asked for God's wisdom and guidance as we weighed the pros and cons of each option.

Brandon's parents are incredible people. In many ways, they are no different than other parents. The major difference I saw between them and many parents I have worked with was their complete and total determination to put emotions aside and do what was best for Brandon and their other two sons. They weren't concerned with possible embarrassment they would face as people found out about their son's behavior. They also were not trying to protect their son from suffering consequences for his actions. When parents try to protect themselves from embarrassment and their wayward teenager from suffering, they completely handicap the process and significantly limit their options. Usually status quo or worse is the result.

Another important point that Brandon's parents understood was the need to protect the well-being of the siblings in the home as decisions were being made. Their lives are at stake as well. How we handle situations with older kids will determine the course of the younger siblings' lives – good or bad. Brandon's parents fully understood that important aspect of their decision.

Brandon's mother got real busy researching options for temporarily sending Brandon away. She ended up being an expert on the different programs that are available for troubled teenagers. At the same time, they were giving Brandon an opportunity to get back on track without having to leave. With the support of our counseling sessions, Brandon's parents agreed to have a session where they listened to Brandon's thoughts and opinions on what he believed he needed from them. The freedom he missed the most was the ability to drive. The parents agreed to give him back that freedom with specific limits and requirements agreed to by Brandon. He was told that he had to inform his parents of his whereabouts at all times, keep his cell phone turned on and answer it any-time they called, and that he was only allowed to go where they gave him permission to go. And the single, biggest deal breaker was that there was not to be any indication of the use of illegal substances, including alcohol. If there was, the deal was off. Brandon agreed to all of their conditions and the driving restriction was lifted.

This was Brandon's chance to prove to his parents that he could live within their limits and monitor himself without having to leave the public school he professed to love. His parents had laid out very clearly which behaviors would be a problem. There was no ambiguity or mixed messages. They allowed him to see his girlfriend, but within the limits they set. Brandon left that counseling session with a smile on his face and a cheerful attitude. Within two weeks, he was back in my office with his parents, angrier than I had ever seen him.

At the beginning of this session I required Brandon to take off his sunglasses. He refused. I told him that if he didn't remove them, I would assume that he was high. He still refused. I allowed him to speak first. All he had to offer were emotional statements about how much he hated his parents and his brothers. He had turned 17 recently, so I asked him why he continued to live with them if he hated them so much. I offered the suggestion that he move out and get his own place or move in with a friend. He admitted that he didn't want to do that. He couldn't give a reason why. This was very important information. He was conflicted and still loved and wanted to be with his family. I was sure of that.

This kid was stuck between a rock and a hard place and was unable to extricate himself. He was miserable. The only people he could safely lash out at were his parents because he knew they would always love him and never reject him, no matter what he said or did. It was up to his parents to extricate him and give him a chance to reclaim his life. They were up to the challenge.

Brandon's mother had found, in her hours of research, an amazing residential facility halfway across the country that was recommended by Focus on the Family. They set their minds and hearts on getting their son there and proceeded to take steps to make it happen. He was told that he was going to have to go somewhere, because his current behavior and continued illegal activities would not be allowed to continue in their home. He tried and tried to talk them out of it and promised over and over to obey their rules. Their decision was confirmed as the right one when one evening Brandon told his dad that he would do anything they asked of him to get to stay home. Not 10 minutes later, his dad told him to get off the computer and go to bed. Brandon refused and started yelling at his dad - not 10 minutes after promising to comply with whatever they asked of him.

Brandon's parents quickly lined up admission and financing for the residential facility. They informed Brandon of where he was going the night before he was scheduled to leave. He was given an opportunity to pack whatever he wanted to take. Most of what he packed (electronics) was taken away when he got to the facility and sent back home with his parents. At the facility, he was not allowed communication with anyone from home except his parents, through his counselor. The program included intensive counseling, group sessions, year-round school and physical work. Spiritual growth is the top priority in everything they do at this particular facility. Since Brandon has been at the residential facility, his parents have endured his begging, pleading and promises as he has attempted to change their minds and be given permission to come home. They have remained determined that he is going to complete the yearlong program, even though it means spending his senior year at the facility. It also has been a tremendous financial sacrifice for them as they have been forced to make major changes in their lifestyle, dip into their retirement savings, and borrow money to make this happen. They are more concerned with Brandon's spiritual, emotional and psychological well-being than with the things that our culture values. They realize that they have this small window of opportunity to influence Brandon's life in a way that can put him back on the narrow path. Once he has turned 18 and graduated high school, their ability to make decisions on his behalf will be gone. They are also determined that their younger two sons and their family as a whole will not be sacrificed on the altar of Brandon's issues and destructive choices. They completely and totally trust God with their lives and with Brandon's life.

I recently spoke with Brandon's parents. Brandon had earned the right to come home for a brief visit at the halfway point in the program. They allowed him to have his girlfriend visit him at their house and had a relatively pleasant weekend before Brandon had to return to the facility. You may think that this is not a success story since in some ways it looks like Brandon's parents just gave up and sent him away. Actually, the exact opposite is true. Giving up is when we throw up our hands and allow our teenagers to completely disrupt our home and engage in dangerous behaviors, to the detriment of the whole family. Giving up is when we look the other way and allow our teenagers to hang out and party every weekend with peers. Giving up is when we look the other way and just hope for the best when we know our teenager is sexually active.

No one knows how Brandon's life will go once he gets out of the program. There's one thing of which we can be absolutely sure. Brandon will always know that his parents were willing to do whatever it took and make whatever sacrifice was necessary to give him every opportunity to turn his life around. What he does with that opportunity is between him and God.

I hold these parents up to you as role models. The fact that Brandon's father did not withdraw or avoid this difficult situation was critical to the outcome. Many times, this father physically stood between Brandon and his mother to take the slings and arrows that were intended for her. Brandon's mother stood strong when she felt like crumbling. She didn't say "wait till your father gets home." She stood up to Brandon when she was the only one there but allowed her husband to take the lead when he was there. They worked as a team and didn't turn on each other. They kept their focus on Brandon and his issues and didn't back down. What a beautiful example of team parenting and marriage partnership. This is how it is intended to work!

If your mind is going to places where you are assigning blame for why Brandon began having problems, stop right there! It is so easy to say, "Well, these parents made a mistake when they homeschooled Brandon through 8th grade. He was too sheltered and couldn't handle the real world." Or some might say, "They never should have put him back in public school. Public school is to blame!" Beating up on the parents or rehashing past decisions is not useful when a family is at a crisis point with their child. Each and every situation is unique. There are kids who do fine in public school all the way through. I know one family whose kids were homeschooled through middle school then excelled when they entered public high school.

There is rarely one single place to lay blame. If only it were that simple. The blame game in the middle of a crisis is a pointless diversion. Often one parent turns on the other in the midst of the crisis, which only serves to derail the process. It is so important to stay focused as parents when your child is at risk. Keep your marriage together if at all possible. If you are already divorced, work together as parents if you possibly can. If not, find someone who will walk with you through the crisis. Ask God for wisdom and guidance every day, have high expectations of your children and do what you believe is right for your children every moment of every day. Parent boldly and sacrificially and trust God with the outcome.

CHAPTER 14

PSYCHIATRISTS AND MEDS

I f you have an adolescent or teen in your home with behavioral issues, especially in school, you are most likely familiar with the mental health system. This system is our culture's answer to the behavioral issues plaguing our children and teenagers. A parent's first introduction to this system is usually through their child's public school. A teacher or guidance counselor experiences behavioral issues with a child and makes a recommendation to the parent that they take their child to see their physician, a psychiatrist, or a psychologist for an evaluation. In most cases, the child is initially evaluated for Attention Deficit/Hyperactive Disorder (ADHD). If the problem is defiance, the child will most likely be given a diagnosis of Oppositional Defiant Disorder (ODD). Sometimes a child will leave the initial evaluation with a diagnosis of both ADHD and ODD. Rarely does a child or adolescent leave a psychiatrist's office without at least one prescription in hand.

My opinion and experience with the system as it currently functions is somewhere in the middle between "wonderfully effective" and "hideously destructive." Personally, two of my four children have ADHD, so I know that it is a very real disorder and that appropriate medications can be life-changing for some children and teens. I'm not so sure about ODD. Of the dozens of children and teens who have come into my office with this diagnosis, only one, in my opinion, truly fit the criteria. In my professional experience, I have seen both of these diagnoses given on more than one occasion without the child having met the diagnostic standards presented in the *Diagnostic and Statistical Manual (DSM)*.[139]

I do not fault psychiatrists for all the problems with the current system, just as I don't fault teachers for all of the problems with the educational system. Psychiatrists are working within guidelines determined by non-clinical, clerical types at insurance companies who require a numerical diagnostic code before they will pay for services. I get that. However, the vast majority of psychiatrists I have encountered professionally just seem to go with the flow. Kids and teenagers are processed in and out of their offices in fifteen minute intervals with prescriptions flying off prescription pads so fast it's no wonder there are long waits at the local pharmacy.

I want to clarify that there are two psychiatrists I have encountered in our region who, I believe, have shown tremendous restraint and professional ethics in spite of the system they are working within. They have given me hope that there are many others like them. They insist on giving each patient as much time as they need, they make eye contact and really listen to what the patient and the parent have to say, and they don't always write a prescription. Because of how they function, they probably personally make less money than psychiatrists who cram in as many patients as they can in a day. Both of these psychiatrists are willing to collaborate, and actually seek out collaboration, with the therapist when making diagnoses and monitoring meds. It has been quite heartening to work with both of these professionals and I believe the collaboration has been very effective in helping patients and their families. Isn't that what it's really all about?

****

I believe that parents and the educational system often share responsibility and accountability for the dysfunction of the current mental health system. When a child or adolescent demonstrates defiance or an inability to function as expected in the classroom, so many parents look for a cause outside of their or their child's realm of responsibility. Isn't it easier and doesn't it feel better to be able to blame a disorder for our child's unacceptable behavior? If a psychiatrist or physician says that a disorder is to blame and a pill is the fix, doesn't that allow the parent to leave the doctor's office with their self-esteem intact? Wouldn't we rather see our child as the innocent victim of a disorder than an out-of-control troublemaker?

By the same token, teachers and schools have discovered within this system an easy out that saves them a lot of trouble and money dealing with difficult students. These students run the gamut from those who just can't sit still and keep their mouths shut to those who demonstrate aggressive defiance. Once again, the teacher is spared the challenge of finding ways to modify the classroom or the mode of instruction for the student who can't sit still. The educational system has reached a point where their hands are tied when it comes to dealing with aggressive defiance. Remember the story in an earlier chapter about the school system that dared to require a haircut? They were raked over the coals by the media as though asking a parent to keep their child's hair out of his eyes is way out of line. Sometimes the only options left for school administrators in dealing with an aggressive child is to call in law enforcement or turn the student over to the mental health system. There exists in our region of the country a system of alternative schools and classrooms that quite often simply babysit the most defiant children. These kids grow up to become defiant and under-educated adults.

It seems to me that we, as a culture, have willingly jumped on this bandwagon of mental health diagnosis and meds in a feeble attempt to deal with the downward spiral of behavioral problems in this generation of children. I would speculate that the trend toward fixing our problems with a pill or drug began with the generation of the 60's. The drug culture of the 60's was bound to permeate our society as those who grew up during that time took over leadership in every area of our country.

As I discussed in the chapter on drugs, many of today's adults have smoked marijuana since their teenage years. I believe that we are experiencing the effects of the long-term use of marijuana in the attitudes and perspectives that have taken hold in America. Our cultural attitudes so often mimic the attitudes commonly seen in addicts. The most pervasive of the similar attitudes that I have witnessed include the need for a quick fix for emotional pain, a refusal to accept personal responsibility in relationship, a lack of sacrificial commitment in relationship, the need to blame others when things go wrong, an avoidance of emotionally difficult circumstances, a lack of willingness to persevere in unselfish or sacrificial tasks, the need for tangible, immediate rewards, and a very short attention span. If the adults in our culture are comfortable with drug use, the mental health profession will most definitely reflect that attitude. It makes perfect sense that drugs would be seen as the solution to the behavioral issues we are experiencing with our children and teenagers.

****

Given the reality of how the mental health system currently functions, my recommendation to parents who believe that their child needs mental health intervention is to see a competent family therapist first. A good therapist is going to spend time getting to know the child or teenager and their family system. They will be equipped to perform a thorough evaluation of the child and if psychiatric intervention is warranted, the therapist can recommend a competent psychiatrist and collaborate with them in the best interest of the child and family. Sometimes changes can be made within the family system in therapy that removes the need for psychiatric intervention.

Of course, if a child or teenager at any time expresses a desire to hurt themself in any way, they must be immediately transported to the nearest hospital emergency room and assessed for crisis intervention. If the child is uncooperative, the police and ambulance attendants must be allowed to forcibly transport the child. Always take any threat of self-injury seriously and act upon it immediately, even if the child begs you not to take them to the hospital. If your child threatens to kill themself and you believe it is merely an attempt at manipulation, have them transported to the hospital anyway. If you are right, the teenager will have learned that it is not acceptable to ever make such a threat unless they genuinely need help. If a teenager has a tendency to have suicidal thoughts, they must be encouraged to tell someone so that they can get the care they need. One of the reasons teens often give for not telling an adult about self-destructive thoughts is that they feel badly about disrupting the family. As difficult as it is to hear that your child is having suicidal thoughts, your child must be reassured that their well-being is your top priority. If a child or teenager seems to lose touch with reality in any way, they must be immediately transported to the hospital.

****

I want to be very clear that I believe in psychiatry. I am very thankful that we have access to competent psychiatrists in America and that prescription drugs are available to help us when we need them. I also believe, however, that we must practice psychiatric and pharmacological intervention in the lives of children and teens with greater care and caution than our mental health system currently exhibits and our schools typically encourage. I believe that in most cases these interventions should be used as a last resort and always in conjunction with talk therapy.

CHAPTER 15

HOW DO I GET MY GROWN KIDS TO GROW UP?

I have told many people that letting go of my adult children was harder than having a house full of young children. I was not at all prepared for this process and how emotionally difficult it would be. For me, there was a distinct moment in time for each of our children when I experienced emotions as if a part of me was being ripped away from my body. Over the years I let go of Chris in stages, but a little part of me was still holding on. We allowed him to live with us for one year after college then set a deadline and he moved out. The final stage of emotionally letting go came at a time when God made it very clear that I had to get out of the way so that He could work in Chris's life. It required a physical and emotional separation from Chris. I had many sleepless nights crying and pouring out my heart to God during that time. A peace then settled over me as I completely let go of Chris and put him in God's hands.

For Rebecca it hit me as she was planning her wedding. I cried uncontrollably for about two days. There was nothing anyone could do to console me. It was a necessary emotional release. It was actually kind of comical when it hit me with Rebecca. Paul, Michelle and Heather were trying to console me so they took me to see a matinee of the latest Veggie

Tales movie then to Chick-fil-A for lunch. I wore sunglasses in the theater and cried through the entire movie (which is hard to do when you're watching Veggie Tales surrounded by a bunch of giggling preschoolers), then I cried as I ate my Chick-fil-A nuggets (which is also hard because they're so delicious). Michelle had enough of my emotional indulgence and launched into a stern lecture about how I needed to pull myself together. In the middle of her scolding, I suddenly realized how funny the situation was and began laughing. Of course, that got Michelle laughing too. When we finally stopped laughing, it was over.

I believe letting go is a necessary part of parenting. It might sound like I'm contradicting my previous advice about boldly intervening in our kids' lives, but this chapter is specifically about children who are 18 or older and have graduated high school. I don't think we stress enough how important this letting go is to the health and well-being of our adult children. They may seem ambivalent about the process, but we must let go anyway and sometimes a little push out the door is required. If parents don't let go, strong-willed children will often do whatever is necessary on their part to force the issue. If the parents still refuse to let go, the adult child may continue to live in their parents' home and eat their parents' food, but they will make their parents' lives miserable. If your adult child is living in your house and you find yourself in constant conflict with them, they need to be pushed to leave the nest. Help them plan their departure, but make it clear that their departure is imminent. Setting a deadline is often very effective.

If this developmental stage is not allowed to successfully transpire, more compliant, sensitive kids will give up rather than risk emotionally devastating their parents. Depression almost always follows when compliant adult children give up and accept responsibility for their parent's emotional well-being. It is sad to see these adult children who have decided to accept being attached to their parents for life, or at least for the foreseeable future. Many of them live with their parents well into adulthood and fail to establish their own families.

I've known young men who live with their parents and have a woman living with them in their childhood bedroom. Some of these young men will have children with women they never intend to marry and attempt to parent these children from their own parents' home. In some cases, the grandparents end up doing most of the parenting chores with their grandchildren because their own children never transitioned to adulthood. As I mentioned before, this phenomenon is sometimes called 'boomerang' kids, because they often leave for college or get their own apartment temporarily only to move back in with their parents when they fail to emotionally separate.

The complete and total responsibility for the failure to emotionally separate lies squarely on the parents. It is the last real responsibility we have for our children. It is irrelevant whether our kids want us to let go or desire to move out of our house. We must require them to get out on their own. Parents must allow their daughters to grow up and resist the temptation to baby them or attempt to run their lives. Young men need to be pushed out of the house as soon as they have the capability to get a job and support themselves. That doesn't mean that they need to have enough money to support themself at the same level of comfort that you have provided them. I recently had two sets of parents tell me that their adult children couldn't move out because they were saving up until they could buy a house. These young adults were attempting to avoid the struggle of working their way up from first apart-ment to first house. What a shame! There is so much to be learned and experienced and self-esteem to be developed through that struggle!

If adult children refuse to get a job or some sort of post-high school education or drag out the educational process, they need to be given a deadline and forced out. It's for their own good. We must not allow our adult children to become comfortable living in their childhood bedroom or in our base-ment. Some young people use the excuse of student loans or some other kind of debt as a reason they have to live with their parents. That excuse doesn't fly. Where did we get the notion that we are responsible for our adult children until they can make a seamless transition into the equally comfortable lifestyle of which they are accustomed? Once again, we are falling into the trap of helping our kids avoid any sacrifice or challenge. As a result, we are protecting them from the very experiences that will develop maturity in them and shape them into godly men and women. Having loans to pay off just means they will have to live in a less expensive apartment or maybe have a couple roommates. It might be a little difficult for them. They may experience some challenges, discomfort and even unhappiness. They will grow through it!

We must remember James 1:2-4:

"Consider it pure joy, my brothers, whenever you face trials of many kinds because you know that the testing of your faith develops perseverance. Perseverance must finish its work so that you may be mature and complete, not lacking anything."[140]

Take away the trials of many kinds and guess what? You end up with a person who never becomes mature and complete. We as parents often enable our adult children to avoid trials of many kinds. We will be required to answer to God for that someday. When your child reaches adulthood, his life and choices are between him and God. Get out of the way!

****

The other pitfall we must avoid as Christian parents is allowing our adult children to have someone of the opposite sex sleep over or share their living quarters in our home, unless they are married and in the process of moving into their own place. As long as a person lives in their parents' home, no matter how old they are, the parents' rules must still be respected and followed. If your son or daughter refuses to comply with your rules, they need to leave immediately. Don't compromise your beliefs for your adult child's comfort, even if they are paying rent to you. Your beliefs and convictions should not be up for sale. They can set their own rules when they are paying for and living in their own home or apartment.

I think sometimes we make excuses to allow our kids to stay in our home because we can't imagine not having them under our roof. It is definitely a transition for parents and children. For some people this transition is easier than it is for others. Not only are our adult children making a developmental transition, but we are facing a developmental transition as well. The parent's transition is into the "empty nest" stage of life. I understand how difficult this transition can be. For single parents or mothers who have not worked outside the home, it can seem like jumping off a bridge into an abyss of loneliness and insignificance. However, no matter how difficult it is to make this transition, emotionally disabling our adult children to spare ourselves the pain of this transition is absolutely unacceptable. It has been very difficult for me personally to envision a life with no children living at home. I have absolutely loved being a mother. The most fun I have is being involved in some activity with my children. It is extremely difficult for me to have that stage of my life coming to an end. As I write this, all four of our children and their respective spouses live at least 30 minutes away from us. One of our children lives 2000 miles away and one of them lives in another country. They have very busy lives so we don't see them as much as we would like. However, I am so very proud of all of them and the way that they have created their own amazing lives of purpose. For Paul and I, this is the next stage of life that holds new growth and challenges and is part of God's plan for all parents.

****

If we think about parenting from God's perspective, we must accept the fact that our children are not given to us to be our possessions used for our own selfish purposes. They do not belong to us, they belong to God. God places children in our lives and gives us the responsibility to love and train them so that they become men and women who love and follow Christ and His purpose for them. It's a huge responsibility. Of course, we derive enjoyment and fulfillment from raising our children and we love them in a way that we love no one else. The love between parent and child is intended to model the love God has for us, His children. Family is a gift from God. When it works the way God intended, it is a beautiful entity like no other and provides a loving support system to walk with us through this life. It is not intended to be an excuse for holding people in emotional bondage.

When we truly love our children in the sacrificial way that God intends, we will always put their best interest above that of ourselves. Letting go means a huge life change for parents, but we can be assured that successfully letting go will free our children to be everything God intended for them to be. Our role becomes a supportive one as we are there when they ask us to listen or give advice with no emotional strings attached. Our children should never be made to feel that they are responsible for our emotional well-being. That will keep them in bondage like nothing else.

I believe that successfully letting go sets up an opportunity to embark on a whole new adult-to-adult relationship with our children. It may not happen right away, but it can develop into something beautiful over time. I did not let go in the best possible way with my older two children but I sure did learn a lot through the process. I am convinced that refusing to let go will cause the parent/child relationship to deteriorate into resentment, hostility and disrespect. We must cooperate with and encourage the natural process so our children can successfully transition into adulthood. We can learn a lot from mother birds who put thorns in the nest when the time is right for their babies to leave the nest. We must figuratively put thorns in the nest when our children become young adults.

Most parents these days line the nest with downy soft feathers, making their adult child's life so comfortable at home that they lose all motivation to leave. The most loving thing we can do for our adult children is to encourage them to leave and develop a life separate from us. Actually it is our responsibility.

****

So, what do we do about a wayward adult child? (Now remember, we are talking about adult children.) It is so difficult and gut-wrenching to watch a child who we poured our life and love into from birth turn his or her back on everything we taught them. It feels personal. It happens even to parents who were diligent and faithful in their parenting. It's a matter of free will on the part of the child. We have free will until the day we die and no matter how faithful our parents were, we can still choose to throw it all out the window and follow a different path. The converse is also true. Some adult children become devout Christians in spite of the fact that they had irresponsible, absent or abusive parents. All we can do as parents of wayward children is to pray every day for them. We must not try to control them, scare them or guilt them into returning to the faith. If we parented to the best of our ability, they know what we believe. It is up to us to resist the temptation to enable them or intervene in their lives. When we stay overly involved in the lives of our adult children in an attempt to direct them back to the right path, we only give them reason to push away even more.

Often times parents will call their adult children almost daily, even when they are married, and in every conversation question and pressure them about their lack of church attendance or some other issue they feel is important. They mean well and are genuinely concerned about their children but this approach doesn't work and only makes adult children dread and avoid their parents' phone calls. We must allow our adult children to see clearly where they are headed, without our intervention. If you've been even a halfway decent parent, your adult child already knows exactly what you think about any given subject. Let your kids go, get out of God's way and pray for them. God is much better equipped to intervene in their life and change them at the deepest parts of their being. Give advice when it is sought. The rest is between them and God.

****

The parable of the Prodigal Son found in Luke 15:11-32 in the Bible has so many important lessons for us as parents of adult children.[141] I encourage you to read it once again. Let's dissect this parable and see what we can apply to this subject. The Father in the parable is representative of God and both sons are representative of us, His children. I believe that the relationship that God has with us is a perfect example which we should strive to emulate as parents. Therefore, I believe we can apply the lessons of The Prodigal Son to our own situations with our adult children.

In this parable, the younger son demanded that his Father give him his share of the family's estate. The Father did exactly that. Then the son collected his belongings and took off. There is no mention of him discussing his intentions with his Father or being appreciative for what his Father had given him. There were no tearful goodbyes. It seems pretty clear to me that this son was rebellious and I think we can assume that this rebellion didn't just appear overnight. The fact that the Father responded to the demands of his son so quickly indicates that this was not a new attitude on the part of the son. This son seems like the type who had given his Father trouble in the past, possibly for many years. So, do we see the Father begging, pleading, yelling, barricading the door, guilting his son into staying or refusing to give the son his inheritance so that he is manipulated into staying? No. This Father gave his son what was his, without making a scene, and LET HIM GO! I'm sure the Father knew that his son would squander his inheritance and not make good decisions and most likely end up in a bad situation. He let him go anyway.

The story goes on to detail how the son traveled to a distant country and "squandered his wealth in wild living."[142] Guess what happens next? There's a famine and suddenly the son realizes that he has no money and can't even buy food to keep himself alive. Did the Father orchestrate this famine and the consequences that the son experienced? No. Did the Father run around trying to bring about situations that would cause the son to come to his senses? No. Did the Father send his servants to tell the son how his behavior was causing his Father to have health issues and sleepless nights in an attempt to manipulate the son into returning home? No. Did the Father continue sending money to the son so that he would never experience hardship or suffering regardless of his irresponsible actions? No. Did the Father call in a favor of a fellow wealthy landowner to get his son a job? No. The answer to all these questions is no. The Father stayed home and continued going about his business because he had let go of his adult son. The Father removed himself from the situation his son had created and allowed his son to experience the natural consequences of his own actions.

So didn't this Father care about his son? Wouldn't he have done something if he cared? When the son came to his senses and decided to come home, where was the Father? He was watching for his son's return.

"But while he was still a long way off, his Father saw him and was filled with compassion for him; he ran to his son, threw his arms around him and kissed him."[143]

If the Father saw him a long way off, he had to be watching for him, day after day. He saw his son returning the minute his silhouette could be seen on the horizon. The Father's reaction shows that he was longing for his son's return. You can almost see the son, weak from hunger and filthy from living with pigs. His defiant will was broken as he dragged himself back home with his head hanging. What did the Father do? He didn't even hesitate. He ran the long distance to meet him, threw his arms around him and kissed him. He didn't say "I told you so." or "Boy do you stink!" or "It's about time you came home. Do you know what you've put us through?" He wasn't angry or resentful or bitter that his son had taken off like he did and squandered his money. He was filled with love and compassion and welcomed his son back again

Most often, when we hear the parable of the Prodigal Son, it is in the context of God and his wayward children. It is a beautiful description of how God feels about us and treats us when we return to Him. God allows us to find our own way, even if it means we suffer consequences for our decisions, but He is always watching and waiting for our return. He doesn't hold grudges or feel a need to punish us when we return. His love and forgiveness are always waiting for us. However, I also see an application to our situations as parents of young adult children who rebel, take off and squander their lives. God gives us a very clear picture of how we are to respond when they leave, while they are gone, and when they return. He knows exactly how we feel as heartbroken parents and He will walk with us through that most difficult time.

CHAPTER 16

SUGGESTED SOLUTIONS FOR AMERICA'S EDUCATIONAL SYSTEM

I t is important that we understand and accept that educating children is not the number one priority of teachers' unions. Unions represent the teachers and administrators in public schools. They will promote governmental decisions that first and foremost keep them in their position of power and secondarily keep teachers and administrators in their positions of power. If a conflict arises between an approach that will improve the educational environment for our children or the best interest of teachers and administrators, the unions will come down on the side of protecting teachers and administrators every time. They may not outright admit to this bias, but they don't need to. Their role is the same as any other labor union – to represent the best interest of the laborer. Therefore, I am not so inclined to blame the unions for the problems in public education today. The problem lies with society and government expecting the labor unions to fight for the best interest of the children and giving away the power to the unions to determine what's best for the education of our children.

If you have the resources, private schools offer an option for educating your child that does not usually involve extreme changes in the life of the family (beyond financial). However, often there is very little difference between public and private schools, except maybe class size. Our two older children switched over to a private Christian school when Rebecca was in 6th and Chris was in 8th grade. It wasn't perfect but it was an improvement over dealing with the issues that were plaguing our son in public school. We gave Rebecca the option and she chose to attend the small private school as a personal preference. Both Chris and Rebecca flourished in private school.

Michelle and Heather attended public school through 10th grade, then switched to one of our state's cyber charter schools and graduated from the cyber charter school system (the first one like it in the country). This cyber school is considered part of the state public school system but all of their schooling was done online from home their junior and senior years. Some subjects were covered in a virtual classroom and some were self-paced. It was a huge change from the large, traditional public school system they were in from Kindergarten through 10th grade, but they adjusted well and accepted full responsibility for their education. I believe that online schooling prepared them for college and life in many ways. Their standardized test scores improved, especially in math. The "New York Times" recently ran an article online that quoted research as showing that "On average, students in online learning conditions performed better than those receiving face-to-face instruction."[144] I'm not surprised by this finding.

****

"U. S. News and World Report" published an editorial written by Editor-in-Chief Mortimer B. Zuckerman in their September 2009 issue that defines the situation and offers a solution regarding public education in America. The article states the shocking statistics that in America:

"Just 71 percent of students graduate from high school within four years. And the numbers for minorities are worse: 58 percent for Hispanics and 55 percent for African-Americans."[145]

Zuckerman states that "There is unanimous agreement on what the key is: better teachers."[146] He makes his point with the statistically-supported fact that "There is more variation in student achievement between classrooms in the same school than there is between schools."[147] He proceeds to suggest a solution that would require fewer teachers, modify their role, and provide for more consistency in education. He describes a solution which has been successfully implemented in India and is presented in the book *Liberating Learning: Technology, Politics, and the Future of American Education*[148] as follows:

"We would escape geography by using the technology to have the best teachers appear in hundreds of thousands of disparate classrooms. . . . The classrooms would be equipped with a large, flat-screen monitor with white-boards on either side; the monitor would be connected to a school server that contains virtually all of the lessons for every subject taught in the school, from kindergarten through 12th grade. The contents would use animation, video, dramatization, and presentation options to deliver complete lessons, to convey ideas in unique ways that are now unavailable in conventional classrooms. The classroom teachers would play the role of enhancers, answering questions and helping students better under-stand the material covered electronically; they'd pause the presentation to ask questions and to prompt critical thinking. The whiteboard would be the platform for student involvement."[149]

I find this proposed solution to be a fascinating, intelligent and bold response to the current state of affairs in most schools in America. If you dissect this proposal, you see several ways that it addresses problems that teachers face in the typical American classroom.

The classroom structure proposed by Zuckerman would take away the burden carried by individual teachers to prepare lesson plans and come up with new and creative ways to keep the attention of their students. The lessons would be consistent in classrooms across the country, so children in poor school districts would receive the same education as students in wealthy districts, and poor districts would have the same access to specialized academic subjects, such as foreign languages, and special education classroom instruction. The same technology that keeps children and teenagers mesmerized for hours playing video games or watching music videos would hold their attention in the classroom. The class period would be tightened up so as to allow very little time for students to become distracted or create conflict. The teacher would no longer be the focal point of the classroom which would potentially dissipate some of the power struggle between student and teacher. The teacher would assume a support role so that they would not be the one doing most of the talking front and center. This would take them somewhat out of the line of fire and the focus would be on the monitor in the front of the classroom. A fast-paced, multi-faceted, dynamic presentation would command the attention of students. Short quizzes would randomly pop up throughout the lesson to keep kids on their toes. The teacher would have the ability to pause the presentation if questions arose.

Of course, some students will continue to sit in the classroom text messaging their friends or sleeping. My feeling is that this type of behavior needs to be reported to parents. If parents don't take action to deal with these behaviors, the student should be allowed to fail the class. If students engage in behaviors that disrupt or distract other students, and continue after one warning, they would be isolated (with a teacher in the room and a surveillance camera in use) in a special detention classroom for the rest of the day with no access to their cell phone. Their lunch would be brought to them. They would not be allowed out of detention until they satisfactorily completed the class work they missed. Most students want to be with their peers. At the very least, the students who want to learn would not be disrupted in the classroom and other students would take note and not disrupt because they would not want to be isolated. My belief is that if we present dynamic lessons to teenagers in a way that stimulates their thought processes then engage them in relevant discussion about what they have learned, many currently bored students will come alive and engage in the process.

****

Another method of educating our children is through a voucher system. Basically, a voucher worth a certain amount of money is made available to students who qualify based on standards set by the state in which they reside. That amount of money can be applied to their child's education at the institution of their choosing. It's a shift in the way the state spends their educational dollars. The money is attached to the child and goes with the child instead of the money going to the school. Schools then are forced to compete for the students and the educational dollars.

A voucher system was established in Washington D.C. in 2004 which offered qualified, low-income students up to $7,500 per year toward their education. Teachers unions and other education groups have fought against voucher programs in court and by lobbying political leaders. However, a 91% graduation rate was reported in 2009 among the more than 3,300 recipients of the D.C. vouchers.[150] In May 2009, President Obama stopped new students from entering the program by cutting off funding; however, the program was reinstated by Congress in 2011 to the delight of parents. "Andrea Thomas, a 27-year-old mother of two from LeDroit Park, was jubilant. . . "We got the scholarship back!" she said. "They tried to take it from us."[151] Another mother who was applying for vouchers for her children said of her local D.C. public school: "There

233

were kids getting beat up on the way home. I said to myself, "That's not going to happen to my child.'"[152] This same mother had been awarded a voucher six years earlier for her older daughter. That daughter had used the voucher to attend a private Catholic school where she excelled. She is currently a sophomore in college.[153]

The state of Louisiana recently opened up the application process for their statewide *Louisiana Believes* voucher plan.[154] It will be interesting to watch how this voucher program changes the educational outcomes in Louisiana, whose students consistently rank near the bottom educationally when measured against students in other states.

The point of voucher programs is obviously to allow low-income families the option of removing their children from failing schools and sending them to successful public or private schools instead. Wealthy families have always had that option. It has been middle class and low income families who have most often been stuck sending their children to failing public schools. It is easy to see why teachers' unions fight against vouchers. Vouchers take the power and money away from the public schools and put it into the hands of the parents. In a voucher system, public schools are made to compete. It's no longer an educational monopoly. This type of competition is bound to be a win/win as failing public schools will have to take a good hard look at themselves and find ways to improve in order to retain students.

****

Of course, homeschooling is still a very positive option for educating our children. Depending on the state in which you reside, there are homeschool groups which provide much needed support, including tutoring and social functions. It is a myth that homeschool children grow up to be socially backward. It is the rare homeschool parent who keeps their children closed up in the house never allowing them to socialize. The main reason parents make the tremendous sacrifices required to homeschool their children is because they care so deeply about the well-being of their children. These parents desire to raise well-rounded, healthy children. They just do not believe that sending their children into today's public school system will achieve that goal. There are different types of socialization – some good and some bad. Not all socialization is a good thing. As I mentioned earlier, my sister has homeschooled all five of her children and has made sure that they are involved in community sports programs and church activities with their peers. They have also had friends in the neighborhoods they have lived in. Her children have had very active social lives. Other homeschool parents I have encountered are very much like my sister. They are just willing and able to take the full responsibility for educating their children, which not all parents are willing and/or able to do.

****

As Christian parents, we must not sit on the sidelines in the educational debate. We must pray long and hard when deciding to whom we entrust the education of our children. As parents, God has given us the primary responsibility for educating our children so we must oversee their education very closely and we must take full responsibility for providing their moral and spiritual education. The days of sending our children off to the local public school and Sunday School classes on Sunday and believing we have done our duty as parents are long over. That false sense of security is part of the reason that so many children who grew up in Christian homes are now wandering from the faith. We, as parents, send our children off and expect someone else to train them instead of taking responsibility for actively training them ourselves. Many of us have abdicated that responsibility and it's time for us to take it back!

SECTION THREE

CLOSING THOUGHTS

CHAPTER 17

ARE YOU FEELING HOPELESS?

I have no doubt that many parents who pick up this book are feeling completely hopeless. This world offers very little hope or encouragement when our children turn on us and become self-destructive. Often the world is encouraging our children to continue further down the negative, destructive path that they are on. Nothing crushes a parent's spirit more deeply than the constant fear that a police officer is going to show up at the door to say that their child is either arrested, in the hospital or dead. Also, nothing hurts more deeply than having the child that you poured your life and love into from infancy, acting and speaking as though they absolutely despise you. I have personally experienced both of these scenarios. The sense of hopelessness experienced by many parents can feel as desperate as if they were on the Titanic sinking into the cold, dark waters of the Atlantic Ocean with no hope of rescue in sight.

So let's imagine that you and I are on the Titanic and the ship is going down. I tell you that I have one lifeboat, it is the only way you can be saved from drowning and I am offering you hope in what seems to be a hopeless situation. I tell you that there is no other way to survive the sinking of the ship. All you have to do is acknowledge that you believe me by accepting the gift of your salvation with a grateful heart and you will be rescued from certain death. But let's say you respond to my offer by telling me that you don't accept the idea that this one lifeboat is the only way and you are determined that there are other ways you can be saved. After all, it isn't fair that there is only one way, so you are going to try to figure out another way on your own. Also, you add that you happen to be a very good swimmer so you'd rather just take your chances with everyone else on the ship and try to save yourself. We know what happens next. You go down with the ship and with everyone else who refused the same offer of salvation.

We are all on the Titanic of life and God is offering each of us a lifeboat. All we have to do is believe Him and accept it. However, many of us reject God's offer of salvation through Jesus' agonizing death on the cross. He took the punishment for all the sin ever committed. He offers salvation and wants every one of us to accept it so that we can be made righteous in the sight of a perfect God. That is the first step you must take to enter into a new life of miracles, because "with God, all things are possible."[155]

As parents, we all face times when we need a miracle – when we have come to the end of our own resources and have absolutely nothing left to give. Even in the most desperate times, if we accept God's offer of hope He walks through it all with us. We are never alone. One of God's greatest gifts to parents is the gift of supernatural wisdom promised in chapter one of the book of James in the *Bible*. All we, as followers of Jesus Christ, have to do is ask for wisdom and God gives it to us. The wisdom of God is beyond human knowledge and understanding. It shows us the way when life is cloudy and confusing.

Hope is waiting for you to open the door to a life where all things are possible. My deepest desire is to give you that gift of hope through Jesus Christ. This hope is supernatural and it comes from believing in and surrendering your life and your children to God. I have witnessed more miracles in my counseling office than I can count because God has inter-vened in the lives of families. But He only intervenes when we invite Him.

It is very important that you understand that your prayers will only reach God if you have gone through His Son Jesus Christ (He is that one lifeboat). Jesus made it as clear as possible when He said "I am the way, the truth and the life. No one comes to the Father except through Me."[156] The Bible also says that "Salvation is found in no one else, for there is no other name under Heaven given to men by which we must be saved."[157] If there was any other way to God, Jesus wouldn't have gone through what He did when He gave up His life on the cross to cover our sins. When Jesus was in the Garden of Gethsemane before He was arrested, He asked God if there was any other way. The answer was no.[158] If it was possible for us to be good enough by our own efforts or if any other religious leader in history could save us, Jesus wouldn't have had to go to the cross. We don't like to be told that there is just one way to do something. We want to make our own way or pick the way that we decide is best for us. But Scripture is clear – there is no other way. Instead of being angry that there aren't other ways, thank God for making a way and for the gift of hope!

Once you have told God that you accept His gift of salvation through the death of Jesus Christ and ask Him to forgive your many sins, the Holy Spirit comes to live inside of you, literally. He speaks truth and comfort to your heart and your spirit. You are now free to let go and give yourself, your marriage and your children to God. He created your child in the first place and loves him or her even more than you do. God offers His supernatural wisdom and guidance every day. All we have to do is ask. By reading Scripture, we are encouraged and given strength and peace, no matter what our circumstances. Your perspective will change and you will learn to lean on God and draw on His strength to get through every day. I have personally experienced being carried by God through extremely difficult circumstances when I would have given up and fallen apart if I was relying on my own strength.

God values us and has a significant purpose for everyone, male and female. If you are unfulfilled in your life, God has the answer. He has an amazing, unique plan and purpose for every single person who ever lived and He will bring it about if you will follow Him. God also lays out a way of life that protects us from emotional, physical, and psychological devastation and leads to real pleasure, intimacy and fulfillment. It's not too late to point your children and teenagers to the source of true peace, joy and fulfillment in every area of life. Demonstrating this type of focus in your own life is the most effective way to influence your children to do the same.

I want you to experience the power of God in your life, as I and many others have. God knows and cares about what you're going through and He knows your children better than you do. He is able to speak to your son or daughter in the depths of their heart and intervene in their life in ways that you and I can't. Give God a chance. You have nothing to lose and everything to gain! He's just waiting for you to ask!

ENDNOTES

[1] Dr. James Dobson, *Dare to Discipline*, (Wheaton, IL: Tyndale House Publishers, 1970), 22-23.

[2] Ibid., 23.

[3] Genesis 8:21.

[4] Jeremiah 17:9.

[5] Taylor Caldwell, *On Growing Up Tough,* (Green-wich, CT: Fawcett Publications, Inc., 1971), 55.

[6] Acts 17:28.

[7] James 1:5.

[8] Deborah Huso, "One In Four Teenage Girls Has STDs," http://www.lymebook.com/fight/1-in-4-girls-have-stds/ (Nov. 26, 2009).

[9] "Genital Herpes – CDC Fact Sheet," www.cdc.gov/std/herpes/stdfact-herpes.htm (January 31, 2012).

[10] "Millennials Losing Faith In God: Survey," http://www.huffingtonpost.com/2012/06/05/more-millennials-losing-their-religion_n_1571366.html (June 5, 2012).

[11] Joseph A. Califano, Jr., *High Society: How Subs-tance Abuse Ravages America and What To Do About It,* (Jackson, TN: PublicAffairs Press. 2007).

[12] Sam Cooper, "In life, it's all about the first five years," http://www.theprovince.com/life/life+about+first+five+years/3688534/story.html (March 21, 2011).

[13] I Thessalonians 6:18.

[14] Jessica Bennett & Jesse Ellison, "A Case Against Marriage," *Newsweek Magazine*, June 21, 2010, 43-45.

[15] Mike and Harriet McManus, *Living Together Myths, Risks and Answers,* (New York, NY: Howard Books/A Division of Simon & Schuster. 2008), 60-61.

[16] Libby Quaid, "Sexting Common Among Teen-agers," *The York Daily Record,* December 4, 2009.

[17] Naomi Wolf, *Is Porn Driving Men Crazy?* http://www.huffingtonpost.com/naomi-wolf/post_2186_b_892185.html *(July 7,* 2011).

[18] Ibid.

[19] Ibid.

[20] Kerby Anderson, *A Biblical View on Homosexua-lity,* (Eugene, OR: Harvest House Publishers, 2008).

[21] Hebrews 4:15.

[22] James 1:13-15.

[23] I Corinthians 10:13.

[24] I Thessalonians 6:18.

[25] Genesis 37-50.

[26] I Thessalonians 5:22.

[27] Jeremiah 29:11.

[28] John 10:10b.

[29] Brian Hiatt, *Paul McCartney: Yesterday & Today,* http://www.rollingstone.com/music/news/paul-mccartney -yesterday-today-20120618 (June 18, 2012), 2.

[30] "DrugFacts: Marijuana," www.nida.nih.gov/Infofacts/mari-juana.html, (January 12, 2007).

[31] Ibid.

[32] Ibid.

[33] *Saturday Night Live,* NBC Television.

[34] James 1:4.

[35] Psalm 1:2b.

[36] Philippians 4:8.

[37] II Corinthians 10:5.

[38] Dr. Richard Marks, Mastering Life Ministries, www.marriageforlife.org

[39] Ephesians 5:18.

[40] Bristol Palin and Nancy French, *Not Afraid of Life: My Journey So Far.* (New York, NY: HarperCollins Publishers, 2011), 49.

[41] James 1:2-4.

[42] Chris Prentiss, *The Alcoholism and Addiction Cure,* (Los Angeles, CA: Power Press, 2007), 121.

[43] Ibid., 122.

[44] Joseph A. Califano, Jr., *High Society: How Substance Abuse Ravages America and What To Do About It,* (Jackson, TN: PublicAffairs Press, 2007).

[45] Ibid.

[46] Davis Guggenheim and Billy Kimball, *Waiting for Superman,* Distributed By: Paramount Vantage, Directed By: Davis Guggenheim, Produced By: Lesley Chilcott, (January 22, 2010).

[47] Michael Goodwin, "Teachers' latest free ride," http://www.nypost.com/p/news/local/teachers_latest_free_ride_12Bmli0oszgm2Autt4FUBJ (February 19, 2012).

[48] Davis Guggenheim and Billy Kimball, *Waiting for Superman,* Distributed By: Paramount Vantage, Directed By: Davis Guggenheim, Produced By: Lesley Chilcott, (January 22, 2010).

[49] Ibid.

[50] Steven Brill, "The Rubber Room: The Battle Over New York City's Worst Teachers," http://www.newyorker.com/reporting/2009/08/31/090831fa_fact_brill (August 31, 2009).

[51] Davis Guggenheim and Billy Kimball, *Waiting for Superman,* Distributed By: Paramount Vantage, Directed By: Davis Guggenheim, Produced By: Lesley Chilcott, (January 22, 2010).

[52] Steven Brill, "The Rubber Room: The Battle Over New York City's Worst Teachers," http://www.newyorker.com/reporting/2009/08/31/090831fa_fact_brill (August 31, 2009).

[53] Davis Guggenheim and Billy Kimball, *Waiting for Superman,* Distributed By: Paramount Vantage, Directed By: Davis Guggenheim, Produced By: Lesley Chilcott, (January 22, 2010).

[54] Jonathan M. Seidl, "Michigan Education Official: Educators, Not Parents Know What's Best For Kids' Education," *The Blaze.com,* (February 14, 2012).

[55] Davis Guggenheim and Billy Kimball, *Waiting for Superman,* Distributed By: Paramount Vantage, Directed By: Davis Guggenheim, Produced By: Lesley Chilcott, (January 22, 2010).

[56] Dan Lips, Shanea Watkins, Ph.D. and John Fleming, "Does Spending More on Education Improve Academic Achievement?" *Backgrounder, No. 2179,* (Washington, DC: The Heritage Foundation, September 8, 2008).

[57] Ibid.

[58] Betty Friedan, *The Feminine Mystique*, (New York, NY: W. W. Norton & Company, Inc., 1963), 15.

[59] Ibid., 32.

[60] Ibid., 15.

[61] Ibid., 15.

[62] Jessica Bennett & Jesse Ellison, "A Case Against Marriage," *Newsweek Magazine*, (June 21, 2010), 43-45.

[63] Ibid.

[64] Betty Friedan, *The Feminine Mystique*, (New York, NY: W. W. Norton & Company, Inc., 1963), 15.

[65] Judith S. Wallerstein, Julia M. Lewis, and Sandra Blakeslee, *The Unexpected Legacy of Divorce,* (New York, NY: Hyperion, 2000), xxxii.

[66] Ibid., xxxiii.

[67] Ibid., 295.

[68] Ibid., 297.

[69] Ibid., 272.

[70] Acts 20:35.

[71] I Corinthians 13:4-7.

[72] Matthew 7:12.

[73] Rick Warren, *The Purpose Driven Life*, (Grand Rapids, MI: Zondervan Publishing Co., 2002), 17.

[74] Kevin A. Hansen, "I wish I could go back. . . Confessions of a Divorced Mom." http://www.huffingtonpost.com/

kevin-a-hansen/confessions-of-a-divorced_b_1631504.html (July 3, 2012).

[75] "Genital Herpes Statistics," http://www.herpesclinic.com/genitalherpes/genitalherpesstatistics.htm

[76] Deborah Huso, "One In Four Teenage Girls Has STDs," http://www.lymebook.com/fight/1-in-4-girls-have-stds/ (Nov. 26, 2009).

[77] Ibid.

[78] Nick Vujicic, *Life Without Limits*, (Colorado Springs, CO: WaterBrook Press, 2010), 40.

[79] Ibid., 40.

[80] Ibid., 111-117.

[81] Tom Henderson, "Author Urges Parents to Quit Hovering," http://www.parentdish.com/2009/09/29/author-urges-parents-to-quit-hovering/ (September 9, 2009).

[82] Lenore Skenazy, *Free-Range Kids, Giving Our Children the Freedom We Had Without Going Nuts with Worry,* (San Francisco, CA: Jossey-Bass/John Wiley & Sons, 2009).

[83] Tom Henderson, "Author Urges Parents to Quit Hovering," http://www.parentdish.com/2009/09/29/author-urges-parents-to-quit-hovering/ (September 9, 2009).

[84] Ben Carson, MD, *Take the Risk*, (Grand Rapids, MI: Zondervan Publishing Co., 2008), 7-8.

[85] Ibid., 194.

[86] Stephanie Elliott, "Are You a Helicopter Parent?" http://www.babyzone.com/mom/motherhood/helicopter-parents_83221 (March 24, 2013).

[87] Ben Carson, MD, *Take the Risk*, (Grand Rapids, MI: Zondervan Publishing Co., 2008), 72.

[88] Ibid., 73.

[89] Ibid., 75.

[90] Ibid., 87.

[91] Dictionary.com, "Boomerang Kid," "http://dictionary.reference.com/browse/boomerang+kid (March 24, 2013.

[92] Genesis 39:6.

[93] Genesis 39:9.

[94] Genesis 39:20b-21.

[95] Jeremiah 29:11.

[96] Hebrews 13:8.

[97] Genesis 50:20.

[98] Dr. James Dobson, *The New Strong Willed Child Workbook,* (Wheaton, IL: Tyndale House Publishers, 2005), 5.

[99] Ibid., 5.

[100] Proverbs 22:6.

[101] The NET Bible, *Bible.org,* http://www.netbible.com

[102] The NET Bible, "Proverbs 22:6," http://net.bible.org/#!bible/proverbs+22:6 Translation Notes.

[103] James-Michael Smith, "Train up a child?" *Methodist Examiner,* http://www.examiner.com/article/train-up-a-child-2 (June 3, 2009).

[104] Ibid.

[105] The NET Bible, "Proverbs 22:6," http://net.bible.org/#!bible/proverbs+22:6 Translation Notes.

[106] Matthew 7:13-14.

[107] The NET Bible, "Proverbs 22:6," http://net.bible.org/#!bible/proverbs+22:6 Translation Notes.

[108] Barna Group, "Evangelism Is Most Effective Among Kids," http://www.barna.org/barna-update/article/5-barna-update/196-evangelism-is-most-effective-among-kids (October 11, 2004).

[109] Substance Abuse and Mental Health Services Administration (SAMHSA), Office of Applied Studies, "Underage Alcohol Use: Findings from the 2002-2006 National Surveys on Drug Use and Health," http://www.oas.samhsa.gov/underage2k8/toc.htm (June 26, 2008).

[110] Sam Cooper, "In life, it's all about the first five years," http://www.theprovince.com/life/life+about+first+five+years/3688534/story.html (March 21, 2011).

[111] Jessica Keller, "May you be covered in the dust of your Rabbi," http://jesskeller.wordpress.com/2012/06/28/may-you-be-covered-in-the-dust-of-your-rabbi/ (June 28, 2012).

[112] Ephesians 6:17.

[113] Matthew 19:26.

[114] Gary Martin, "Spare the rod and spoil the child," *The Phrase Finder,* http://www.phrases.org.uk/meanings/328950.html

[115] Proverbs 13:24.

[116] Proverbs 23:13-14.

[117] Galatians 5:22-23.

[118] Galatians 5:24.

[119] Psalm 23:4.

[120] Psalm 100:3.

[121] John 10:11.

[122] Hebrews 13:20.

[123] I Peter 5:4.

[124] Galatians 4:6.

[125] Phillip Keller, *A Shepherd Looks at Psalm 23*, (Grand Rapids, MI: Zondervan Publishing House, 1970).

[126] Ibid., 93.

[127] Ibid., 94.

[128] Ibid., 95.

[129] Ibid., 98.

[130] Dr. James Dobson, *The New Strong-Willed Child*, (Carol Stream, IL: Tyndale House Publishers, Inc., 2004), 154-155.

[131] Amy Noall, "Why children need boundaries," *Family & Parenting*, http://www.examiner.com/article/why-children-need-boundaries (November 17, 2009).

[132] Rick Warren, *The Purpose Driven Life, (Grand Rapids, MI:* Zondervan Publishing Co., 2002).

[133] Richard Primason, Ph.D., *Choice Parenting.* (iUniverse Publishing, 2004).

[134] Genesis chapters 6-9.

[135] Exodus 20:15.

[136] P. A. Alberto and A. C. Troutman, *Applied Behavioral Analysis for Teachers (7th ed.),* (Upper Saddle River, NJ: Prentice Hall, 2006), 12.

[137] Raymond E. Fancher, *Pioneers of Psychology,* (New York, NY: W. W. Norton & Company, 1979), 364.

[138] Meg Meeker, MD, *Strong Fathers Strong Daughters. 10 Secrets Every Father Should Know,* (New York, NY: Ballantine Books, 2007).

[139] *Diagnostic and Statistical Manual of Mental Disorders Fourth Edition,* (Washington, DC: American Psychiatric Association, 1994).

[140] James 1:2-4.

[141] Luke 15:11-32.

[142] Luke 15:13.

[143] Luke 15:20.

[144] Steve Lohr, "Study Finds That Online Education Beats The Classroom," *New York Times: Bits,* http://bits.blogs. nytimes.com/2009/08/19/study-finds-that-online-education-beats-the-classroom (August 19, 2009).

[145] Mortimer B. Zuckerman, "Technology as Our Teacher," *U. S. News and World Report,* (Sept. 2009 Vol. 146 Issue 8), 104.

[146] Ibid.

[147] Ibid.

[148] Terry M. Moe and John E. Chubb, *Liberating Learning: Technology, Politics, and the Future of American Education,* (San Francisco, CA: Jossey-Bass, 2009).

[149] Mortimer B. Zuckerman, "Technology as Our Teacher," *U. S. News and World Report,* (Sept. 2009 Vol. 146 Issue 8), 104.

[150] Robert Samuels, "Parents rush to apply for D.C. private school vouchers," http://articles.washingtonpost.com/2011-06-25/local/35233856_1_voucher-program-private-school-vouchers-parents-rush (June 25, 2011).

[151] Ibid.

[152] Ibid.

[153] Ibid.

[154] "Louisiana Voucher program opens," *KNOE.Com,* http://www.knoe.com/story/18592618/louisiana-voucher-program-opens (May 22, 2012).

[155] Matthew 19:26.

[156] John 14:6.

[157] Acts 4:12.

[158] Matthew 26:36-46.

CPSIA information can be obtained at www.ICGtesting.com
Printed in the USA
LVOW13s1542121113

361026LV00002B/437/P